CHRISTIANITY AND ISLAM

THE BIBLE AND THE KORAN

CHRISTIANITY AND ISLAM

THE BIBLE AND THE KORAN

FOUR LECTURES

REV. W. R. W. STEPHENS

GYAN

Published by

Gyan Publishing House
5, Ansari Road
Daryaganj, New Delhi-110002
Phone: 011-47034999, 9811692060
E-mail: books@gyanbooks.com

Distribution Network
gyanbooks.com
India, USA, Canada, UK, Australia, France

ISBN: 978-81-212-9416-4 (PB)
First Published, 1877

2nd Impression 2023

Printed at: Gyan Press, Delhi.

CHRISTIANITY AND ISLAM

AUTHOR: W. R. W. STEPHENS

CHRISTIANITY AND ISLAM.

THE BIBLE AND THE KORAN

CHRISTIANITY AND ISLAM

THE BIBLE AND THE KORAN

FOUR LECTURES

BY THE

REV. W. R. W. STEPHENS

PREBENDARY OF CHICHESTER: AUTHOR OF 'THE LIFE OF S. JOHN CHRYSOSTOM
MEMORIALS OF THE SOUTH SAXON SEE' ETC.

NEW YORK
SCRIBNER, ARMSTRONG & CO.
1877.

PREFACE.

The following Lectures were in substance delivered during Advent, last year, in the Cathedral Church of Chichester. They have been prepared, with some alterations and additions, for publication, in compliance with the wish of some who heard them, and in the hope that they may prove a contribution, however humble, to an intelligent appreciation of the great subject with which they deal. The annual delivery of a set of lectures in the Cathedral is one of the conditions on which my Prebendal Stall has been held since its foundation in the thirteenth century, and

I selected Christianity and Islam for my subject last autumn, believing the consideration of such a subject to be especially salutary and opportune at the present time. If the Eastern Question has its roots to a large extent in religious differences between Mussulmans and Christians, it behooves us all, and more particularly the theological student, to ascertain as exactly as possible what those differences really are; how far they are deep and vital, how far superficial and incidental, what practical difficulties they place in the way of Christian and Mussulman living together on terms of amity; how far, and in what way, these difficulties may be surmounted.

To the great prophet of Arabia, and to the marvellous work which he accomplished, I have endeavoured to do justice, in opposition to the false and calumnious estimate which in a past age condemned Mahomet himself as a kind of malicious fiend, and his religion as a diabolical invention. On the other hand, I have sought to show that Christianity and Islam are radically diverse in the nature of their origin, in the character of their sacred books, and in their practical effects upon mankind; that the difference between them is one not of degree, but of kind, according to the wise saying of Dr. Arnold, that while other religions showed us 'man seeking after God,' Christianity showed us 'God seeking after man;' a maxim which students of the crude science of comparative religion are too apt to forget. I have endeavoured, lastly, to point out that if there be these real and vital distinctions between the two religions, it is worse than folly to try and ignore them; that while there ought to be, and might be, peace and goodwill between the believers in rival creeds, it should not be placed on a rotten foundation;

the rotten foundation which would be laid by those who see imaginary resemblances, and are blind to real distinctions; for if indiscriminate antagonism is mischievous, indiscriminate concession is mischievous also, and can only lead to confusion and disaster.

I subjoin a list of the principal authorities which I have consulted:—

The Koran, translated by *Sale*, with introduction and notes.

Gibbon, 'Decline and Fall,' ch. l., li., liii.; written in his most brilliant and masterly style, only too much coloured by the sarcasms in which he indulges in the treatment of any religious subject.

Milman, 'Latin Christianity,' Book IV. ch. i.

Dr. White, 'Bampton Lectures;' fairly represents the narrow estimate of Mahomet prevalent in the last century.

Sir W. Muir, 'Life of Mahomet' (four vols.); learned and impartial, as well as reverent and Christian in tone.

Weil, 'Mohammed der Prophet;' full and learned, and more readable than

Sprenger, 'Life of Mohammed;' which is equally, if not more learned, but less impartial and more theorizing—'more Germanico.'

Bosworth Smith, 'Mohammed and Mohammedanism;' able and ingenious, but the partiality of the author for Mohammedanism seriously detracts from the accuracy and value of the work.

J. H. Newman, Lectures on the Turks, in 'Historical Sketches.'

E. A. Freeman, 'Lectures on the History and Conquest of the Saracens.'

G. Finlay, 'History of Greece under Foreign Domination,' vol. i. (2nd edition); a most invaluable work.

W. G. Palgrave, 'Central and Eastern Arabia.'

Sedillot, 'Histoire Générale des Arabes' (2d edition); this did not come into my hands soon enough to be of much use to me, but it seems full of most interesting matter, put together in a very pleasant way.

Articles in the 'Christian Remembrancer,' for June 1855; in the 'North British Review,' for August 1855; in the 'British Quarterly,' for January 1872; in the 'Quarterly,' for January 1877, but this last was too late to be of any service to me.

CONTENTS.

CHRISTIANITY AND ISLAM.

LECTURE I.

THE ORIGIN OF CHRISTIANITY AND OF MOHAMMEDANISM. SKETCH OF THE LIFE AND CHARACTER OF MAHOMET.

Some said "He is a good man:" others said, "Nay, but he deceiveth the people."

IT will be my endeavour in this set of lectures to gather up the principal points of contrast between Christianity and Islam, the Bible and the Koran; between the religion founded by Jesus Christ and the religion founded by Mahomet—between the book which contains, as the Christian believes, the word of God; and the book which contains, as the Mussulman no less believes, the words of God conveyed through the mouth of His prophet.

I use the word contrast advisedly, in preference to the word comparison. The difference between the two terms is this: To contrast is to place two things, which have some resemblances to each other, side by side, in order to detect the points of unlikeness. To compare, on the other hand, is to place two things, which present some dissimilarity, side by side, in order to find out the points of likeness. If two things are exactly alike, there is, strictly speaking, no comparison between them; they are practically identical. If, again, two things are utterly and totally unlike, they cannot fairly be contrasted. It is possible, for instance, and may be instructive, to contrast a man with an ape, because amidst many differences there are some resemblances between the two animals. But to contrast a man with a fish, or still more with some inanimate object, would be an idle task, because where nearly all is difference, there are no points to contrast.

The advantage, then, of contrasting is to bring out (where this is desirable) into prominent relief the differences between two objects which in some respects are similar. And I think that an investigation, by this method, of the vital differences between Christianity and Islam is not unprofitable in the present day. Up to at least the beginning of this century the character of Mahomet and of the work which he accomplished was unfairly depreciated. In the pages of Prideaux, of Dr. White, and to some extent even of Gibbon, he is represented as a consciously designing and artful impostor, who pretended to be the recipient of divine revelations merely in order to facilitate his schemes of personal ambition. This view of Mahomet's character has now been abandoned as untenable by all sound critics. But in the eagerness of a better informed and more enlightened age to redress the balance, the danger is that it may be overweighed in the opposite scale. The character of the great prophet of Arabia and of his religion will now no longer be underrated; the fear is lest by many they should be painted in colors too attractive.

It is difficult to doubt that other motives also, besides the praiseworthy desire of repairing past injustice, operate in the same direction. This is not the time to minutely examine the causes which alienate many in the present day from the Christian faith. With some it may be the bewilderment of the understanding through the manifold difficulties supposed to be experienced in reconciling the discoveries of science or criticism with Holy Scripture; with others it may be that hardening of the spirit against the reception of spiritual doctrine, which is one natural consequence of spending life in the midst of material luxury; with others it may be the aversion of a selfish and impure heart from submission to the severe moral standard of the Gospel: with others it may be that tendency (natural in an age which has made great advances in knowledge) to independence and conceit, which is inclined to dispute the excellence or truth of most things which our forefathers believed and venerated; with others it may be a mixture of some, or all, of these causes. A fact, however, it remains, that many, in proportion to their disposition to doubt or reject the Gospel of Christ, seem disposed to regard with some favour, even if they do not actually embrace divers forms of philosophy or religion; a favour which to the careful and impartial student seems greatly in excess of the intrinsic merits of those systems. Simple Materialism, Pantheism, Positivism, Mohammedanism, Buddhism, even the gross and (one would have thought) palpable imposture of spirit-rapping, have found their advocates and patrons among men who fancy they discover insuperable difficulties in accepting the faith of Christ as it was once delivered to the saints.

Now, of all the systems here alluded to, Mohammedanism no doubt presents the nearest parallel to Christianity, both in its origin and progress. Its beginnings are not lost in the mists of a remote and fabulous antiquity. It was founded, like Christianity, by one person: this person was at first rejected by his own people; gradually he gathered round him a small band of disciples; out of this germ the faith was propagated which in time won Arabia from idolatry, Persia from Magianism, and wrested some of the fairest provinces from Christendom itself. The sacred book, the Koran, might, in sublimity of language, and, to some extent, even in the purity of its teaching, theological and practical, bear comparison with the sacred writings of Jews and Christians. Finally, the religion thus established has lasted for some 1,250 years, and at the present time maintains its sway over 120 millions or more of the human race. It is the only other religion besides Christianity which inspires its votaries with much proselytising zeal; and in missionary success in some parts of the world, it surpasses its rival. It makes fresh advances every year in Africa, Australia, and the interior of India which exceed the progress of Christianity in those countries.

Such are a few of the salient points of resemblance between Christianity and Islam. But my aim, as was remarked at the outset, is not to compare but to contrast; to discover the differences which underlie the resemblances, and to estimate their importance.

Let us begin, then, with the origin of the two religions, and consider the circumstances under which each was founded, and the character of the respective founders.

It was an observation of Machiavelli that no man could make himself a prince and found a kingdom without opportunities. What were the opportunities of Mahomet? To begin with, what was the state of the world when Mahomet appeared? He was born in the year 570 A.D. The civilised world at that epoch was divided between the two great rival empires of Rome and Persia. Almost incessant warfare was going on between them, and their boundaries were constantly fluctuating. Arabia, being on the confines of the rival powers, was subjugated, so far as the fierce independent spirit of the inhabitants permitted it to be subjugated at all, to each in turn. The religion of the Roman Empire was Christianity; but Christianity on the eastern frontier was distracted and corrupted by a variety of conflicting heresies, which disguised its essential character, and exhausted its vital energy. As the extremities of the human body are the most quickly chilled, owing to their distance from the heart, as the fringe of a garment is the part most liable to be torn and stained, owing to its friction with other substances, so the pulse of national Roman life beat but feebly in the eastern extremities; the eastern fringes of the empire were constantly torn by dissension from the established religion, by revolt against the political government. The associations of their old nationality were too strong for them. Neither the religion, nor the laws, nor customs of the Roman Empire had obtained a firm hold upon them. They were ecclesiastically addicted to heresy—politically addicted to rebellion.

The religion of Persia, whatever it may originally have been, had turned to dualism, or the worship of two co-ordinate powers—the spirit of good or light, Ormuzd; the spirit of evil or darkness, Ahriman. But the Sun being venerated as a symbol of the power of light, a superstitious worship of fire and of the heavenly bodies had practically superseded, to a great extent, the purer and more philosophic creed.

As the Arabs were alternately subject politically to their two powerful neighbours, so did they catch some sparks of the religious spirit prevalent in each. Christianity and Magianism each had their votaries in Arabia, and colonies of Jews had settled there more than 600 years before the birth of Mahomet. But the dominant creed of the Arabs was a kind of degenerate Monotheism; the corrupt offspring of the purer faith of their forefather Ishmael. They believed in one Supreme Deity, but subordinate to Him was a host of inferior divine personages who were supplicated as intercessors. This mixed, mongrel religion had its national home and centre in the sacred temple, the Kaaba, in the sacred city of Mecca. Here was the holy black stone, the relic of an earlier temple built by Abraham and Ishmael, a relic, also, as was believed, of Paradise, where it was originally given to Adam. Once it had been white, but had changed its hue either from contact with sinful lips, or from the repeated kisses of the faithful. There was the print of Abraham's footstep; there was the holy spring, Zemzem, which had burst forth to save Hagar and Ishmael from perishing by thirst. Thither the devout Arab came to worship the God of Abraham, but also to implore the succour of the 360 intercessory powers whose images were ranged within those sacred walls. Round those holy walls he walked seven times, naked, to signify the putting away of his sins. Seven times did he run to and fro between Mounts Safa and Merwa, to typify Hagar seeking water for her child; seven times did he throw stones into the valley of Mina, in memory of the stones which Abraham flung at the Devil, when disturbed by him in the act of offering up Ishmael; for in Arabian tradition it is Ishmael, not Isaac, who occupies the foremost place.

But, shortly before the rise of Mahomet, a spirit of profound dissatisfaction with the national religion had begun to work among the more reflective and discerning of his countrymen. In the introduction to one of the most ancient biographies of Mahomet there is a chapter inscribed 'an account of four men who without revelation perceived the error of idolatry.' This is the substance of it. One day the Koreishites, the tribe which was the guardian of the Kaaba, were celebrating a solemn feast in honour of one of the lesser deities. They bowed the knee before the image, walked round it, and offered sacrifices with customary reverence. But four men secretly held aloof from these acts of devotion, and opened their hearts one to another. 'Verily,' said one, 'our tribe does not know the true religion. They have corrupted the faith of Abraham; they worship a stone and walk round about it, though it neither sees nor hears, and can neither do them good nor harm. Friends, let us seek the truth for ourselves, for verily we are not in the right path.' So they parted and went hither and thither in quest of the pure faith of Abraham. Of the four inquirers, two it is said became Christians; a third after the preaching of Mahomet embraced Islam, but ultimately he too, on going to Abyssinia, was converted to Christianity, and when he met any disciples of the prophet he was accustomed to say: 'We see, and you attempt to see.' The fourth, Zayd by name, renounced and condemned all the gross superstitions of his countrymen, more especially the custom of sacrificing before images, and the horrible practice of female infanticide; but he remained in a sceptical condition of mind, ever longing, but never able, to come to the knowledge of the truth. There is a pathetic story of him in his old age: how he was seen leaning with his back against the wall of the Kaaba, and he cried aloud: 'O, ye Koreishites! by Him in whose hands my soul is, none of you follow the religion of Abraham.' And he continued: 'O Lord, if I knew which form of worship is most acceptable to Thee, I would adopt it; but I do not know it.' Thus he spake, resting his forehead on the palms of his hands. He traveled through Mosul, Mesopotamia, and Syria, seeking repose for his troubled, anxious spirit. In the midst of his wanderings he heard of the growing fame of Mahomet. He started for Mecca, but was murdered on the way.

I have related this narrative, not as considering it in all its details deserving of much credence, but because its very existence, whether true or not, is a proof and illustration of a spirit of dissatisfaction and doubt prevalent at the time to which it refers.

To form any just estimate of the prophet of Arabia and of his work, it was necessary to indicate the conditions, political, social, and religious, of his country.

To sum up, then, Arabia was on the edge of two great rival empires, both weakened by protracted and exhausting contests. The crisis of the struggle, indeed, was contemporaneous with the preaching of Mahomet. Heraclius the Roman Emperor overthrew the Persian power in 629. The Roman Empire was itself weakened in the border provinces by this exertion; the Persian Empire never recovered. The Arabs had been partially subject to one or other power, but never absorbed politically or religiously by either.

Gross superstition and licentiousness prevailed, but a spirit of discontent and skepticism was at work. There was no national unity. Each tribe was a separate independent atom.

The opportunity, then, was favorable for the action of some master mind which should first of all weld the jarring elements of life in Arabia itself into a compact body; then proceed to annex to it the great neighboring Empire of Persia, already prostrate by its rival; and finally to subdue the weakened fringes of that very rival, the Roman Empire.

And this was the work of Mahomet. By bringing men to believe in himself as a divinely inspired prophet, he established a theocracy wherever that belief was accepted; he united his followers under a political and religious system all in one, for the Koran was to them alike their code of civil law and their oracle of theological truth.

Having now examined the nature of the field in which the prophet of Arabia planted his creed, we will turn for a few minutes to the contemplation of the man himself, from the soil to the sower and to the manner in which the seed were sown.

The sketch must of necessity be compressed, but I will try not to omit any incidents of real importance.

Who, then, was Mahomet? Mahomet, the son of Abdallah, and the grandson of Abd-al-Muttallib, belonged to the tribe of the Koreish, the guardians of the Kaaba, and to the family of Hashem, the most honourable family within that tribe.

His father died a short time before his birth. His mother was of a nervous and superstitious temperament. She fancied that about the time of the child's birth she was surrounded by an extraordinary halo of light; and it may have been partly owing to this circumstance that he was named by his grandfather, Mohammed, or "the Renowned." This meaning of the word should be remembered, since it was afterwards turned, as will be seen, to curious account. For the sake of convenience, I follow the more usual European form of the name, and write it Mahomet.

The birth took place at Mecca, on or about August 20, 570 A.D. The child was nursed according to Meccan custom, not by his mother, but by a Bedouin woman, and was reared by her in the desert. When four years old, he had the first of those epileptic fits to which he was liable during all the earlier half of his life. Such fits were regarded with superstitious awe by the Arabs, as the supposed effects of diabolical possession; and, on the recurrence of an attack when he was five years old, the Bedouin nurse took the young Mahomet back to his mother, and could not be persuaded to resume her charge. His mother died when he was six, and his grandfather when he was eight; but he was carefully and kindly brought up by his uncle, Abu Talib, for the duties of a kinsman were scrupulously observed among the Arabs. When he was twelve years old, he accompanied his uncle on a caravan journey to Syria. The story that near Bostra, he made the acquaintance of a Christian monk, tarried with him, and returned under his charge to Mecca, may be true; but it occurs in the midst of such strange tales of incredible wonders that it cannot be accepted as a certain fact. How much of Mahomet's acquaintance with the Gospel history may have been due to this connection, supposing such to have been formed, it is easy to surmise, but impossible in the absence of information to determine. Much more may probably have been learned at the great annual fair held at Ocatz, three days' journey from Mecca, during the sacred month before the pilgrimage to the Kaaba. Here a mixed concourse of Arabs, Christian and Jewish, as well as Pagan, assembled, partly for trade, partly for amusement, partly to engage in poetical and martial contests for prizes. Here, according to tradition, Mahomet heard

Coss, Bishop of Najran, preach on the great facts and doctrines of the Gospel. Here his poetical imagination and patriotic spirit may have been stimulated; here he may have first conceived the ideal of a religion which should combine truths extracted from many diverse sources.

Time went on, and Mahomet became entitled to the enjoyment of a small patrimony, consisting of a house, five camels, a flock of sheep, and a slave. He showed little aptitude for practical business, but was fond of the quiet and innocent occupation of tending sheep, in which he was afterwards wont to compare his early life with the lives of Moses and of David. When twenty-five years old, however, he was entrusted, through his uncle's recommendation, with the conduct of a caravan to Damascus, the property of the wealthy widow Khadijah. He discharged his errand to the complete satisfaction of his employer, who rewarded him with her hand in marriage. She was fifteen years older than her husband; but he remained thoroughly faithful to her, and did not wed another till after her death.

For fifteen years after his marriage—that is, up to the age of forty—Mahomet worshipped the gods of his fathers, but he became increasingly meditative, restless, dejected. He was courteous in company, but spoke little, and with downcast eyes. Gradually he withdrew altogether from worldly business, save such pastoral occupation as milking the goats, or tending the sheep. He spent much time in fasting and prayer in his favourite retreat, a cave on the bare and rugged side of Mount Hira, occasionally even being absent from home all night.

His mind became agitated by doubts respecting the truth of the religion of his forefathers. His seasons of seclusion were more frequent, more prolonged. He renounced the customs which savoured of idolatry.

There are several short chapters in the Koran which probably belong to this period. They read like the expression of an earnest, anxious, inquiring spirit, which has grasped some truths, and is searching for more. The vanity of worldly ambition; the sin of covetousness and slander; the inseparable connection between happiness and virtue, misery and vice; the error of supposing that adversity is always a sign of God's displeasure, or prosperity of His favour; the duty of providing for the fatherless, and of almsgiving; the certainty of future rewards and punishments, according to each man's deeds—these are doctrines insisted upon with the earnestness of profound conviction, mingled with prayers for further enlightenment and guidance.[1]

He was wrought to a high pitch of mental tension, and felt constrained to preach, but he had no commission; he could not point to any credentials to enforce the authority of his messages. By some, indeed, he was respected as a poet or a genius; but by others he was scorned and derided as a soothsayer, a madman, a fool. He began himself to doubt what he was, a

[1] Suras 103, 100, 99, and i.

prophet or a Kahin, inspired by God or by an evil spirit. His wife, his cousin Waraca, and a few other intimate friends believed in his divine inspiration. Such pure conceptions of the Deity, and such a lofty standard of moral teaching and moral conduct, could not, they thought, be the offspring of diabolical influence. When he was yet in the agony of suspense and depression, sometimes even meditating self-destruction, light pierced the clouds. As he was wandering among the solitudes of Mount Hira, he beheld within two bows' length the dazzling figure of the angel Gabriel, and listened with rapture to the memorable command: 'Cry, cry aloud in the name of the Lord; the most merciful God who hath taught the use of the pen to record revelation.'[1] Mahomet hastened home, solaced and encouraged by the assurance that the long-desired commission from on high had come; but for some period, of which the length is uncertain, it was unheeded by all. At last, as he lay one day on the

* [1] Sura, 96.

ground, recovering from one of his fits, and wrapped up in a mantle, he again heard the voice of the heavenly messenger uttering the words: O thou that art covered with a mantle arise, and preach and magnify the Lord, and depart from all uncleanness.'[1]

This is the real starting point of Islam. From this date Mahomet's confidence in himself as the accredited messenger of God never wavers, and all the utterances of the Koran are introduced by the words 'speak,' or 'say,' to intimate that they were put into the mouth of the prophet by his Divine Master. The people, indeed, still demanded some visible evidence of his authority. Let him cause a spring of water to gush forth, or a grove of palms to rise in the desert, or let him ascend to heaven and bring down a book, and they would believe him. But these skeptical taunts no longer harassed the prophet's mind. He could proudly and calmly reply that he was but a man, not empowered to work miracles, but that the divine beauty of his

[1] Sura, 74.

message was its own evidence. It came from God; and, if men did not listen to it, destruction would as surely overtake them as it overtook the cities in the plain.

The work of conversion, however, was slow in its progress. In the course of three years Mahomet had gained about forty disciples, consisting chiefly of his own relations, friends, and dependents. As in the early days of Christianity, so in the early days also of Islam, many converts were obtained from the slave class. The slaves in Arabia were most susceptible of conversion, not only from their position, but also because, being for the most part foreigners, many of them had received a tincture in early life of Jewish or Christian teaching, which rendered them at least averse from idolatrous superstitions. But, as Mahomet's influence increased, jealousy and alarm began to be awakened in the tribe of the Koreish. They were the guardians of the sacred temple, and this heretical son was beginning to shake the fidelity of his countrymen to the ancestral faith, of which that temple was the visible shrine. Some of Mahomet's followers had retired for prayer one day to a valley near Mecca, when a party of unbelieving neighbours unexpectedly passed by. Taunts and retorts led to blows. Saad, one of Mahomet's party, struck an opponent with a camel goad; and this, it was commonly said, was the first blood shed in Islam.

Meanwhile Mahomet waxed bolder. He took up his abode in the house of a convert, named Arcam, hard by the Kaaba, and there he preached, especially at the time of pilgrimage, to all who would resort to him, and seldom without some success. The house of Arcam was the cradle of Islam, as the 'Upper Chamber' in Jerusalem was the cradle of Christianity. The burden of Mahomet's message was the same to all: the absolute unity of God; the authority of His prophet; the moral duties of prayer, almsgiving, and fasting; the certainty of a future state of happiness or woe. The hostility of the Koreish grew more fierce. They seized the converted slaves, and tried to force them to recantation by imprisonment, or exposure to the scorching mid-day sun, and without food or drink upon the gravel of the Meccan valley. Many yielded under repeated application of this torture, but there were others whose constancy was inflexible. No words could be wrung from the slave Bilal in his agony, but 'Ahad! Ahad! one, one only God.'

Mahomet himself was secure under the protection of his uncle Abu Talib. Abu Talib was not a believer in his nephew's mission, but the sacred duty of the kinsman prevailed over all other considerations. 'Beware of killing him,' he said to the leaders of the hostile movement; 'if ye do, verily I shall slay the chiefest among you in his stead.'

For his disciples Mahomet devised a safer means of escape from persecution and possible perversion. By his advice a small party of them sought an asylum in the Christian kingdom of Abyssinia, and their hospitable reception encouraged a larger body to follow their example the year after. This Hegira, or flight to Abyssinia, stands in relation to Islam as the flight of our infant Saviour into Egypt stands to Christianity. It saved the new religion from being crushed in its infancy; and the success of the plan possibly suggested the great Hegira, or migration to Medina some years later. The departure of his converts, however, oppressed Mahomet with a sense of loneliness and isolation, under which his spirits and faith seem for a short time to have given way. Amidst some conflict of evidence something like an inclination to make terms with his opponents seems discoverable. He appears to have uttered words which sounded at least like a concession of some intercessory power to the subordinate deities. But the lapse was of short duration; he was probably soon refreshed by good tidings from Abyssinia (like St. Paul, in his loneliness at Corinth, by the good news which Timothy brought from Thessalonica), and the tone of the Koran waxes louder and sterner than ever, in its denunciation of idolatrous worship. 'Why,' it is scornfully asked, 'implore help from images which have no power to move even the husk of a date-stone?'

The malignity, however, of the Koreish increased in proportion. They tried again to induce Abu Talib to abandon his nephew. The uncle remonstrated with Mahomet for his obstinate persistence in heresy. 'If they brought the sun to my right hand and the moon to my left,' replied the nephew, 'to force me from my undertaking, I would not desist from it until the Lord made manifest my cause, or I perished in the attempt.' But, while inflexible in his purpose, the thought of desertion by his kind protector overcame his feelings, and he burst into tears. The heart of Abu Talib also melted. 'Come back,' he said, 'son of my brother,' as Mahomet had turned to depart; 'go in peace, and say whatsoever thou wilt, for by the Lord I will not in any wise give thee up for ever.'

The Koreish were now thoroughly alarmed,

and, to complete their discomfiture, two new converts were won by Mahomet—Hamza and Omar; men of high position, ability, and influence. Omar had formerly been among his bitterest adversaries. As a last resource the Koreish placed the whole family of Hashem under a ban. The solemn deed of excommunication was hung up in the Kaaba. The Hashemites were assigned an isolated quarter in the suburbs, and all intercourse with them was strictly forbidden. They managed, indeed, to get provisions in by stealth, but were often reduced to great straits for food. The spirit, however, of Mahomet faltered not. At the season of the pilgrimage to the Kaaba, he would boldly enter the precincts and preach, promising temporal dominion and future paradise to all who would become his disciples. But his day was not come, and the people jeered.

The blockade lasted three years (616–619 A.D.). At length some of Mahomet's friends heard that the parchment on which the deed of excommunication was written had been almost devoured by insects. An examination of the document proved the truth of the report. It was represented to the Koreish as a divine judgment cancelling their unbrotherly act. Some of the Koreish relented, and five of their chief men let the Hashemites out of durance, and made themselves responsible for their safety. Fresh troubles, however, were in store for Mahomet. His wise and loving wife Khadijah died, and very soon afterwards his faithful protector, his uncle Abu Talib. Another uncle, also an unbeliever, but with a feebler sense of the duties of a kinsman, promised him protection; but it did not last long, and the situation of Mahomet was again critical.

But new light began to dawn from Medina. Powerful Jewish tribes dwelt there, and in their contentions with Arab neighbours they were wont to say: 'A great prophet shall one day rise among us; him shall we follow, and then we shall overcome you.' Some pilgrims from Medina were attracted by the preaching of Mahomet at Mecca. They said among themselves: 'This surely is the prophet with whom the Jews threaten us; let us then be the first to follow him.'[1] They declared to Mahomet their conviction of the truth of his claims: they promised to enlist their fellow tribesmen in his cause, and to report progress to Mahomet at the next pilgrimage.

A year of anxiety and suspense wore away, and in the spring of 621 A.D. the pilgrims came again. At an appointed spot, the secluded glen of Akaba near Mina, Mahomet sought his friends, and to his relief was greeted by twelve men, disciples, who plighted their faith to him in the simple formula: 'We will not worship any but the one God: we will not steal, nor commit adultery, nor kill our young children; neither will we slander in any wise, and we will not disobey the prophet in anything that is right.' The pilgrims departed, and Mahomet returned to Mecca. He still patiently waited

[1] The dramatic details of this account by Ibn Ishac may not be trustworthy, but they forcibly illustrate feelings which most probably were realities.

his opportunity for decisive action; but the Koran begins to take a wider scope, a sterner, a more defiant tone. The contest between Heraclius and Persia was coming to a crisis; the Koran confidently predicts the triumph of the Roman Emperor.[1] Vengeance is declared as imminent to those who will not believe;[2] a dearth at Mecca is interpreted as a judgment on unbelief, and a call to repentance. Solemn imprecations are invoked by the prophet on himself if the Koran be not a true revelation.[3]

And now another pilgrimage came round, 622 A.D., another meeting in the lonely glen. It was an hour before midnight when Mahomet waited there in a flutter of hope. Presently by twos and threes his converts might be seen stealing from behind the dark rocks into the moonlight, until Mahomet beheld a muster of seventy-three devoted believers in his mission. They spoke in low tones for fear of spies. 'Stretch out thy hand, O Ma-

[1] Sura 30. [2] Sura 21.

[3] Suras 23, 69.

homet,' said Bara, the aged chief of the party; and he stretched it out, and Bara struck his own upon it, as the manner was when one took an oath of fidelity to another, and all the rest did the like. Mahomet chose out twelve of the chief men, saying: 'Moses chose twelve leaders from among his people. Ye shall be sureties for the rest as were the Apostles of Jesus, and I will be surety for my own people.' And all answered, 'So be it.' Thus was ratified the *second pledge of Akaba.*

And now Mahomet felt that the hour was come. The memorable command was issued to his disciples in Mecca: 'Depart unto Medina, for the Lord hath given you brethren and a home in that city.' Gradually the believers stole away. The Koreish were startled day by day to see house after house deserted. In about two months none remained in Mecca except the prophet himself, his faithful friend Abu Bakr, and his nephew Ali. Abu Bakr urged flight, but Mahomet delayed: 'the command,' he said, 'had not yet come from the Lord.' Abu Bakr, however, was determined to be ready when it did come. Two swift camels were bought, and kept tied and highly fed in the yard of his house. A private hoard of money was concealed about his person. The Koreish meanwhile were known to be plotting mischief, and at last Mahomet declared that the decisive hour had arrived. He and Abu Bakr stole away by night, and took refuge in a cave on Mount Thaur, a few miles to the south of Mecca, in order to delude their pursuers, Medina being 250 miles to the north. As they were crouching in the cave, Abu Bakr looking up saw light through a crack in the rock. 'What if the enemy were to spy us out!' he exclaimed; 'we are but two.' 'There is a third,' replied the dauntless prophet, 'God Himself.'

A goat-herd in the employ of Abu Bakr brought them supplies of milk, and on the third day they were informed that the Koreish had abandoned the search after them as fruitless. The daughter of Abu Bakr brought them the two swift camels, and a guide. Mahomet mounted the swifter of the two, Al Caswâ, thenceforward his favourite, and with his friend reached Medina in safety in June 622 A.D., where he was greeted with honour by his new allies, and congratulations by his old disciples.

The Hegira is the epoch in the prophet's career from which his worldly success dates, but it marks the beginning also of a grave deterioration in his moral character. The earnest preacher of a pure theology and a strict righteousness, undaunted in the day of his weakness and danger, becomes in the day of his power a fanatical despot, and is at times cruel with the cruelty peculiar to fanaticism. The single aim of propagating his faith overrides at times all considerations of justice and mercy, and it is often hard to draw the line between religious zeal and personal ambition.

After the flight to Medina the Koran is pitched in a tone of pitiless animosity against the unbelieving Koreish; and the severity of its utterances was matched by deeds of corresponding violence. The prophet would lead the prayers in the mosque, and then conduct a predatory raid upon some caravan of the miscreant tribe. He became a polygamous pope, and the mosque was his St. Peter's and the Vatican in one. Here he preached, here he received embassies, here he planned his campaigns. The Koran, about the fifth year of the Hegira, becomes little better than a military gazette. It announces victories, bestows commendation on their valiant, and incites to further deeds of prowess. A fresh revelation was produced to meet every emergency, removing all obstacles to the advance of the faithful which might arise from a too scrupulous deference to ancient customs, or even to the principles of common humanity and justice. By special divine permission, the sanctity of the month Rajan was violated, which from immemorial antiquity in Arabia, had been consecrated to peace;[1] by special permission captives were executed.[2] Obnoxious unbelievers in Medina

[1] Sura 2. [2] Suras 47, 48.

were assassinated with the connivance, if not by the command of the prophet, and a blessing was publicly pronounced in the mosque by himself on the assassins. By special revelation the destruction of some date trees, which interfered with some military operation of the prophet's, was authorized. By special revelation the marriage of the prophet with another man's wife was sanctioned, and he was exempted from confining himself to four wives, the limit placed by himself on the polygamy of his disciples. The deeds of cruelty which darkened the career of Mahomet at Medina culminated in the cold-blooded massacre of all the men belonging to a hostile Jewish tribe, the Bani Coreitza, and the subjugation of all the women to slavery. To cite the words of Gibbon: 'Seven hundred Jews were dragged in chains to the market-place of the city, they descended alive into the grave prepared for their execution and burial, and the apostle beheld with an inflexible eye the slaughter of his helpless enemies.'

In spite of these repulsive cruelties few will refrain from a feeling of sympathy with the prophet, when the dream of his life was accomplished and his beloved and native city Mecca opened her gates to him. Few will refrain from admiration as they contemplate him gravely and majestically pointing with his staff to the idols which lined the walls of the Kaaba, commanding their destruction one by one, and exclaiming as the largest fell with a crash: 'Truth has come, and falsehood vanishes away.' Few can contemplate without interest mingled with awe, the last days and dying moments of the man who had achieved so great and wonderful a work. Two years only after his reception at Mecca, in the sixty-third year of his age, he was smitten with a mortal fever. He anticipated his end: 'The choice hath been offered me,' he said, 'of longer life, with Paradise hereafter, or of meeting my Lord at once; I have chosen to meet my Lord.' He crawled from his bed one night to select a spot for his burial. For several days he still conducted, but with feeble and fainting strength, the public prayers in the mosque. At last he transferred this duty to his faithful friend Abu Bakr. Yet once more there was a flash of vital energy; he even mounted the pulpit, and, in tones which reached far beyond the outer doors, he called upon the people, like Samuel, to witness that he had not defrauded any, nor taught anything but what God had put in his mouth. This final exertion probably hastened his death. He returned to his bed; he knew the end was near. 'Oh Lord, I beseech Thee assist me in the agonies of death,' he was heard to murmur; and presently in broken whispers, 'Lord pardon my sins . . . . . eternity in Paradise . . . pardon, yes! I come . . . . among my fellow citizens on High.' These were the last words of the prophet of Arabia.

The contrast between the origin of Christianity and Islam is made perhaps sufficiently plain by such a sketch even as I have attempted of the career of Mahomet. Yet it may be instructive to complete and clench this contrast by summing up a few salient points.

Contrast then, first of all, the essentially human character of the career of the founder of Islam with the essentially superhuman character of the life of the Founder of Christianity. Mahomet did not lay claim to the power of working miracles; such as have been ascribed to him bear on the very face of them the marks of being the dress with which the real personality has been clothed by the adoration of a later age. Strip it off, and the true man stands out clear, consistent, and intelligible. You see a bold reformer who in early life rises to the conception of a purer theology and morality than the mass of his countrymen, who gradually persuades himself that he is the depositary of divine revelations, commissioned to unite the manifold and conflicting elements of national life under one simple rigid religious system. There is nothing miraculous in his career, except so far as all genius rises above the ordinary level of character, and produces extraordinary effects.

But in the life of our blessed Lord, the superhuman is of its essence. His birth is superhumanly announced, superhumanly effected. 'He came by a new and living way!' Prophecy upon prophecy, uttered ages before His coming, are fulfilled in the circumstances of His life, even to the most minute particulars. Superhuman He is in deed and in speech every day, although inexpressibly lowly in manner of life. Superhuman He is above all in the hour of death and in the resurrection from the grave. And these circumstances do not belong to the accidents, but to the essence, of the life. Take them away, especially for instance the Incarnation and the Resurrection, and the whole fabric of the life, so to say, falls to pieces. We cannot deal with the history of that life as we can with the history of Mahomet or of Christian saints, round whom a parasitical growth of the miraculous has accumulated, concealing the real shape beneath. We cannot expunge the miraculous from the life of Jesus, and leave a consistent and intelligible residuum. The experiment has been tried, but it breaks down.

The rationalising process which would divest our Lord's life of the miraculous, brings out an irrational result. It leaves us a hazy and shadowy figure, totally inadequate to stand for the founder of a religion which has produced such results as the Rationalist is constrained to admit that Christianity has produced. The phenomena of Christianity remain, but without an explanation. They hang, as it were, in the air, without a foundation to support them.

Take another point:—the moral declension of Mahomet, parallel with the advance of his career. The period when he stands on the highest moral level is early in life. The meditative, musing, retiring shepherd lad, pondering amidst the solitude of his native hills, feeling his way to a purer theology and higher morality than his forefathers, then racked by doubts and fears concerning his mission, then, when convinced of it, calmly and tenaciously adhering to his aim, amidst persecution and distress: this is an interesting, an elevating, and beautiful picture to look at. But of the pure, innocent, kindly youth, very much is effaced in the picture of mingled fanaticism and sensuality which Mahomet presents to us in later years. It is perfectly true that he retained, to the last, many of the simple, frugal habits which were characteristic of his earlier life. To the last he loved to tend the flock and to milk the goats. He was playful and tender in his treatment of children and of his intimate friends. Neither in dress, nor in fare, nor the appointments of his house, did he affect any of the luxury and splendour of an Oriental despot. But the retention of these innocent customs cannot redeem his character from the stains of sensuality and cruelty occasionally very great. Facts are stubborn things, and facts are conclusive on these points. The best excuse for these blots is that Mahomet became a fanatic; and that fanaticism unhinges both the mental and moral equilibrium. To the fanatic the end is everything, and he relentlessly pursues it, without misgivings and without remorse. His moral sense at last becomes so confused and perverted that he gets to think whatever he does in promotion of his one great end must be right.

How far fanaticism itself, or at least the tendency to it, may be due to peculiarities of physical temperament is too deep and complicated a subject to enter upon here. It belongs, indeed, rather to the physiologist than to the historian. It will suffice to remark that in the case of Mahomet there were certainly many symptoms common to his epileptical or hysterical fits, and to his fits of supposed inspiration. Both were generally preceded by great depression of spirits, and accompanied by a cold perspiration, a tinkling or humming noise in the ears, a twitching of the lips, stertorous breathing, and convulsive movements of all the limbs, at times communicated by a kind of electric sympathy even to the camel on which he rode.

The Dervish and Fakir testify to the common Oriental notion that a kind of frenzy or ecstasy must be the natural concomitant of the reception of divine revelation.

The most essential mark of high Christian character is enthusiasm, deep, fervent indeed and intense, but sober in its manifestation. This is only the faint reflex where it is found, of the character of the founder of Christianity. A calm, consistent enthusiasm, to be about His Heavenly Father's business, and to finish the work which was given him to do, constitutes the divine, the matchless beauty of that life. Serenely, he moves on, neither with fanatical haste, nor stoical resolution, but in the unwavering enthusiasm of love to His appointed end—the cross on Calvary, the triumph over death and sin, the accepted sacrifice, the return to the place whence He came. The earthly life rises in grandeur, majesty, and beauty as it advances, not because it is not faultless at the beginning, but because, as it approaches the consummation of the great act to which all the prelude has been working up, it naturally takes a deeper, a more awful tone. It is in the final scene that the superhuman character of the great Actor and of the great tragedy itself, as well as the clear perception of its momentous consequences on the human race, is most deeply impressed upon us.[1] Then it is more than ever that we bow our heads, and exclaim with the centurion: 'Truly this was the Son of God.'

Take another point. In the beginning of his career Mahomet was a preacher of righteousness and of the unity of God, regardless of opposition and danger. He relied simply on the intrinsic merits of his message to make its own way. But, as time went on, he appealed to the pride, ambition, and love of enterprise and plunder inherent in the Arab to promote the propagation of this faith. War, the natural occupation of the Arab,

[1] The popular 'Life of Jesus Christ,' by Dr. Farrar, seems, in our humble judgment, to labour under a fatal defect in failing to bring out this upward, onward, continuous movement: it presents a *series* of brilliant pictures, instead of presenting one great picture.

became invested with a sacred character. Religious zeal and military ardour coalesced in the followers of Mahomet to a degree not equalled in the Scotch Covenanters, or the Ironsides of Cromwell. The joys of paradise were dangled before the eyes of the Mahometan warrior as an incitement to his valour; the horrors of hell were ever urged as a deterrent from faint-heartedness and sloth. In Mahomet's first encounter with the Roman army, one of his soldiers complained of the intolerable heat. 'Hell is much hotter,' was the indignant reply of the apostle. His flight to Medina was a direct renunciation of purely moral and spiritual influence in favour of more material and carnal aids. His entrance into Medina savors more of the political than religious leader. The chief men of the town went out to meet him, and conducted him into it with pomp, riding by his side, and arrayed in glittering armour. The disciples of Mahomet have from that day to this relied largely upon force for the propagation of the faith.

Diametrically opposite to this was the method of the Founder of the Christian religion. The opportunity of His coming was favourable for the assertion of pretensions to temporal dominion. The Jews were fretting under the yoke of foreign conquerors. The least spark would have sufficed to kindle the flame of insurrection. They had persuaded themselves that their Messiah would appear as the champion of their freedom, to restore their long-lost national independence, and to extend the dominion and glory of their empire far beyond the limits reached in the golden days of King Solomon.

The Apostles, even, and familiar friends of Jesus, were affected with this material view of the Messiah's kingdom. We see it in the request of St. James and St. John to sit 'the one on His right hand, the other on His left, in His kingdom.' We see it again in the observation of the two disciples walking to Emmaus: 'We trusted that it had been He which should have redeemed Israel,' implying that His death on the cross was in their view the final frustration of the national hopes. We see it for the last time in the question of the Apostles after the Resurrection: 'Lord, wilt Thou at this time restore the kingdom to Israel?' It was the steadfast opposition offered by Christ to this view of His kingdom, coupled with His searching exposure of national sins, which, humanly speaking, cost Him His life. Had He ever acceded to the Devil's suggestion to command stones to become bread in the sense of using His divine power to obtain material and earthly advantages, or had He yielded to that other temptation to fall down and worship Satan as the price of earthly kingdoms—that is, had He resorted to artifice, to intrigue, to violence—it is plain that He would have been supported by the Jews, and that a worldly kingdom might have been His. Into such snares of the Devil the founder of Islam fell. The power of Mohammedanism as one of the religions of the world dates from the day when Mahomet, *flying* from his enemies, was received by his partisans at Medina with all the honours of a worldly prince. The power of the Gospel dates from the day when its Founder *surrendered* Himself to His enemies saying: 'If ye seek Jesus of Nazareth, I am He;' when He refused to summon legions of angels to His rescue, and was abandoned by all His earthly friends. The power of Islam dates from an appeal to the sword of the flesh: the power of Christianity dates from the day when Christ bade His disciple put up the sword into his sheath, because 'all they that took the sword should perish by the sword.' In the steady decay of all countries under Moslem rule we see the fulfilment of that prophecy. The immediate strength of Mohammedanism is that which ultimately everywhere becomes its weakness—its appeal to material aids for extension and support; its appeal in some degree also to the material and sensual rather than to the spiritual element in the nature of the convert.

Lastly, the character of Mahomet, however much owing to the elevation of his genius, it rises above the ordinary type of his countrymen, is yet as a whole thoroughly Oriental, thoroughly Arabian. Oriental dreaminess, Oriental frenzy, Oriental endurance and fortitude, Oriental sensuality, Oriental despotism, Arabian enterprise, Arabian vindictiveness, Arabian subtlety, all have their place along with higher and nobler qualities in the composition of the great prophet's character.

The pure character of the Founder of Christianity does not bear the mark of any nationality. 'It was constructed,' as has been beautifully said, 'at the confluence of three races, the Jewish, the Roman, and the Greek; each of which had strong national peculiarities of its own. A single touch, a single taint of any one of those peculiarities, and the character would have been national, not universal; transient, not eternal. It might have been the highest character in history, but it would have been disqualified for being the ideal. Supposing it to have been human, whether it were the effort of a real man to attain moral excellence or a moral imagination of the writers of the Gospels, the chances were infinite against its escaping any tincture of the fanaticism, formalism, and exclusiveness of the Jew, of the political pride of the Roman, of the intellectual pride of the Greek. Yet it has entirely escaped them all.'[1] Most true words! To those who would fain expunge the miraculous from the life of Jesus we may well reply there is one miracle which we defy you to remove, and that is the character of Jesus himself. In the literal sense of the expression, 'in Christ Jesus there is neither male nor female, Jew nor Greek, Barbarian or Scythian, bond nor free.' He was the Son of Man because His character was not the offspring of any one race, or caste, or class of men; and we may say boldly that no one could be such a *Son of Man* unless He was also what Jesus declared Himself to be, the *Son of God*.

[1] 'Lectures on the Study of History,' by Professor Goldwin Smith, p. 137.

LECTURE II.

THE THEOLOGY OF THE BIBLE AND THAT OF THE KORAN CONTRASTED.

'Fecisti nos ad Te, et inquietum est cor nostrum donec requiescat in Te.'—AUGUST. *Confess.* i.

BEFORE attempting to draw out the contrasts between the teaching of the Bible and that of the Koran, it may be instructive to notice the differences between the two in their outward form; in construction and style.

What we call 'the Bible,' is in fact a collection of many books. The common use of the word Bible to designate the sacred volume dates, I believe, from the thirteenth century; and we still very often speak of the 'Sacred writings,' the 'Holy Scriptures,' terms which in the earliest ages of the Church were almost exclusively employed. But the name Bible 'the Book,' has become the most familiar, and is perhaps the most precious to us, not only as implying the sovereign supremacy of that book over all other books, but also because it expresses the great truth that although 'the Book' be made up of many parts uttered at 'sundry times and in divers manners,' yet is it after all essentially *one:* inasmuch as the thread of one divine purpose and design runs through the whole. The writings range over a vast space of time, and are cast into a variety of forms—the plain prose of narrative, the poetry of prophecy or praise, the direct teaching of precepts, of exhortation, of reproof, or the more indirect of parable, allegory, or vision. But the ultimate aim of each and all is the same—to conduct men along the stream of God's truth winding its way to the Gospel, as the last and fullest revelation of His love, and to lead them to fall down before Jesus Christ and Him crucified, as the central figure in that final dispensation.

One consequence of the writings which

compose the Bible being cast into such manifold shapes is that the Book becomes in a manner 'all things to all men.' It fits into every fold, so to say, of the human mind and the human heart. It can speak to 'all nations, kindreds, and tongues,' and win converts from all.

In the Bible, then, there is singleness of aim, but variety of expression. In the Koran, on the contrary, there is no continuity of design, but great uniformity in expression. On the one hand it is fragmentary and incoherent; on the other monotonous and level.

The Koran consists of 114 chapters or Suras, each of which pretends to be a verbatim copy of a distinct revelation made to Mahomet. The revelations were written on palm leaves or mutton blade-bones, as Mahomet recited them to his disciples, and were after his death collected into one volume, but without the least regard to chronological order, first by his great friend and immediate successor, Abu Bakr, and afterwards by the Caliph Othman. There is not much more connection between them than between the several grains in a heap of sand, or the several beads on a necklace. There is in the Koran no movement onwards, as in the Bible, from a definite starting point to a definite goal in the history of God's dealings with man. There is no sequence, no coherence between the parts. The perusal, therefore, may be compared, not to the unrolling of a scroll, but to the picking up of scattered leaves, on each of which some distinct oracle is inscribed.

But while there is no continuity, there is, on the other hand, very little variety. Approximate chronological arrangements of the several Suras have been made by Sir W. Muir and others, based on a careful comparison of their contents and style; and from this some variations in their character may be discovered, corresponding with the tone of the prophet's mind, and the circumstances of his life, when they were delivered. But still there is nothing which approaches the many-coloured texture of our sacred volume. Having been all produced within the compass of little more than twenty years, and delivered through one medium, the Koran presents the exact reverse of the 'sundry times and diverse manners' of the Bible. It is all of one time and one manner, and the monotonous reiterations with which the book abounds are exceedingly tedious and dull. Poetry, which sometimes rises to grandeur, alternates with exceedingly dull didactic prose or puerile legend. Of parables there are but few specimens; and these are for the most part borrowed from Biblical sources, and spoiled in transplantation. In the characteristic words of Gibbon, 'the European infidel will peruse with impatience the endless incoherent rhapsody of fable, and precept, and declamation, which seldom excites a sentiment or an idea, which sometimes crawls in the dust, and is sometimes lost in the clouds.' This language is perhaps rather overstrained, and seems to betray the irritation of one who had but recently risen from the irksome task; but it is substantially true nevertheless, and the only other (so-called) sacred book that I have attempted to read which exceeds the Koran in tediousness is the Book of Mormon. That book is much more nearly the audacious travesty of the Bible, which the Koran is not uncommonly called, than the Koran itself. The term 'travesty' indeed is not fairly applicable to the Koran, since it does not appear that Mahomet was well acquainted, if at all, with the canonical books of the Old and New Testaments. There is no evidence in the Koran of deliberate invention; it is rather a badly digested compilation of materials, derived from a variety of sources, true and false, historical and mythical. The Book of Mormon, on the other hand, is a direct, though very tame and feeble, travesty of the Bible in style; and though much of the didactic matter is borrowed from the sacred volume, that which affects to be historical is pure and simple fabrication.

A book, however, which has so long remained an object of veneration to so many millions of the human race as the Koran has remained, must possess some intrinsic merits, some singular power of fascination. These are to be found partly in the great truths which it inculcates (of which more presently), and in the tone of high authority in which they are inculcated, but also partly in the style in which they are expressed. Here, again, the contrast with the Bible is striking and instructive. In the Bible, the matter exceeds in value by a hundredfold the manner in which that matter is expressed. But in the Koran it is to a great extent the other way. Although the exact meaning of a writer must always suffer some detriment by the translation of his thoughts into a language different from that in which they were first conceived and expressed, yet probably there is no book in the world which has lost less by translation than the Bible. This is more especially true of our English translation. The more delicate shades of meaning sometimes disappear, no doubt, in the English translation of the Bible, as they must in the translation of any book; but the *beauty* of the original is rivalled, is often indeed surpassed, by the beauty of the translation. And this is not surprising, when we consider that the Greek of the New Testament, and, though only in some portions and in a less degree, the Hebrew of the Old Testament, belong to periods when those languages were in a state of decadence; whereas the English of the translation represents the golden era of our national tongue, the era of its greatest fertility, and vigour, and grandeur—the era of Spenser, of Shakspeare, and of Hooker.

The Koran, on the other hand, was originally written in the purest Arabic. Mahomet continually appeals to its extraordinary superhuman beauty and purity, as an evidence of the divine source from which he declared it to flow. He challenged unbelievers to produce, even with the aid of genii, any passage worthy to be compared with a single chapter in the Koran. Those who are acquainted with Arabic inform us that in its purest type it is in the highest degree copious, musical, and elegant; and that these qualities all meet in the Koran. Consequently there is scarcely any book in the world which loses so much by translation. The charm of its graceful, harmonious, rhythmical, sonorous sentences utterly evaporates, and the matter, stripped of its gay attire, appears to the ordinary reader insufferably dull and commonplace.

Nothing, however, more forcibly illustrates the poverty of the Koran, viewed as what it claims to be, a complete revelation of theological and moral truths, than its inability to stand the test of translation. If it was really a complete treasury of divine truth, the shape of the treasure-house would be of little importance compared with the jewels it enshrined. But such is not the case; and it is to the consideration of these contents that we now turn: from the form of the book to the book itself.

The Koran may fairly be judged by the definition of its purport as laid down in its own pages. At the close of the twelfth Sura we read: 'The Koran is not a newly invented fiction; but a confirmation of those Scriptures which have been revealed before it, and a distinct unfolding of everything necessary in respect either of faith or practice, and a direction and mercy unto them that believe.' In other words, the Koran claims to be a complete supplement to all preceding revelation, to be the final statement of God's will, both concerning dogmatic belief and practical conduct.

In the remainder of this lecture it is proposed to examine the theological teaching of the Koran by the light of this claim. Does it only confirm the teaching of the Bible respecting the nature of the Divine Being, or does it tell us anything which, supposing it to be true seems an important addition to the knowledge of Mankind concerning the relation of God to man, and of man to God?

The Koran, then, to begin with, teaches a pure, rigid, austere monotheism; a belief in one absolute God, not as a philosophic abstraction, but a living Being, exercising a vital energy upon the world which He has made. The finest passages in the Koran are, undoubtedly, those in which the majesty, and power, and wisdom, of this infinite Being are set forth. Even through the veil of translation some of the grandeur of the original is discernible! For example: 'God! there is no God but He: the living, the self-subsisting: neither slumber nor sleep layeth hold of Him. To Him belongeth whatever is in Heaven or on earth. Who is he that can intercede with Him but through His good pleasure. He knoweth that which is past and that which is to come unto men, and they shall not comprehend anything that He knoweth but so far as He pleaseth. His throne is extended over Heaven and Earth, and the preservation of both is no burden unto Him.'

Or again: 'It is He who hath created the Heavens and the Earth in truth, and whensoever He saith unto a thing "Be," it is. With Him are the keys of the secret things, none knoweth them besides Himself: He knoweth that which is on the dry land and in the sea:

there falleth no leaf but He knoweth it; neither is there a grain in the dark parts of the earth, nor a green thing, nor a dry thing, but it is noted in His clear book. It is He who causeth you to sleep by night, and knoweth what ye merit by day: He also awaketh you therein, that the preordained term of your lives may be fulfilled: then unto Him shall ye return, and He shall declare unto you that which ye have wrought.'

The wonders of the natural world as evidences of the existence and power of a Creator are frequently dwelt upon in language of considerable fervour and force, and at times, doubtless in the original language, of high poetical beauty, *e.g.*: 'Now in the creation of Heaven and Earth, and in the vicissitudes of day and night; in the ship which saileth in the sea laden with things profitable for mankind; in the rain which God sendeth from Heaven, quickening thereby the dead earth; and replenishing the same with all sorts of cattle; in the changes of the winds, and in the clouds that are compelled to do service between Heaven and Earth, there are signs to men of understanding.'

The omnipresence and omniscience of God, and the unerring justice of His future judgment upon men, are declared with earnestness and eloquence. 'There is no private discourse among three persons, but He is the fourth of them; nor among five, but He is the sixth of them; neither among a smaller nor a larger, but He is with them wheresoever they be; and He will declare unto them that which they have done on the day of resurrection; for God knoweth all things.' 'The Lord knoweth the secrets of men's hearts, and there is nothing in Heaven or on earth but it is written in a clear book.' And again, in one of the earliest Suras: 'When the earth shall tremble with her quaking, and the earth shall cast forth her burthens, and man shall say, "What aileth her?" in that day shall she unfold her tidings, because the Lord shall have inspired her; in that day shall mankind advance in ranks, that they may behold their works, and whoever shall have wrought good of the weight of a grain shall behold it; and whoever shall have wrought evil of the weight of a grain shall behold it.'

We may freely acknowledge the beauty and the truth of these and similar passages, and yet heartily concur in the judgment of Gibbon that the loftiest of such strains in the Koran 'must yield to the sublime simplicity of the Book of Job,' and we may well add the Book of Psalms. The mercy and beneficence of God, especially as manifested in His bountiful provision for the physical wants of man, and, on the other hand, the too frequent pride and ingratitude of man in demanding, or expecting as a right, advantages which are conceded only as free and unmerited favours, are topics frequently and powerfully handled, but, again we must say, at a distance vastly below the treatment of such subjects in the Psalms and Prophets of Holy Writ. On the other hand the absolute predestination of men to happiness or misery is repeatedly affirmed with a degree of harshness which it is difficult to reconcile with the attribute of perfect mercy assigned in other passages, and which finds no parallel in the pages of the Bible, where God is represented as a Being, Who, in the beautiful words of our Collect, 'declares His almighty power *most chiefly* in showing mercy and pity.'

Take, for instance, such a passage as this: 'This is a revelation of the most mighty, the *merciful* God, that thou mayest warn a people whose fathers were not warned, and who live in negligence; our sentence hath justly been pronounced against the greater part of them, wherefore they *shall not* believe. We have set a bar before them and a bar behind them; and we have covered them with darkness, wherefore they *shall not* see. It shall be equal unto them whether thou preach unto them, or do not preach unto them; they *shall not* believe.' Or again, yet more boldly; 'Whomsoever God shall please to direct, He will open his breast to receive the faith of Islam; but whomsoever God shall please to lead into error, He will render his breast straight and narrow as though he were climbing up to Heaven:' *i. e.*, attempting an impossible thing.

Place side by side with such passages as these the strongest language to be found in the Bible concerning the impossibility of opening the ears or eyes of some men to the reception of divine truth, and the difference will be at once apparent. In the Koran this impenetrable hardness is represented as the inevitable consequence of an everlasting, immutable decree of God: in the Bible as the inevitable consequence of perverseness and obduracy on the part of man's free will: the working of a natural law whereby powers which are long disused become at last incapable of acting. He who persistently refuses to see or hear God's truth becomes at last unable to see or hear it, just as he who should refuse to move his arm would in time lose all power to move it. This is the import of such passages as 'from him that hath not shall be taken away even that which he hath;' or, 'as they did not like to retain God in their knowledge, God gave them over to a reprobate mind.' Or . . . . 'because they received not the love of the truth that they might be saved, for this cause God shall send them strong delusions that they should believe a lie.' The same meaning underlies those passages also where it is more boldly said that God 'hardened the heart of Pharaoh;' or, 'He hath blinded their eyes and hardened their heart;' or, 'whom He will He hardeneth.' A study of the connection in which those passages occur will always show that such hardening or binding is not arbitrary or initiatory on the part of God. On the contrary it is the judicial penalty of long continued resistance to God's long-suffering efforts to soften the heart and to open the eyes. The design, the desire of God is that 'all men should be saved, and come to the knowledge of the truth:' but man is free: he is not coerced into goodness. God does not reverse His moral law to save a man in spite of himself, any more than He reverses his physical laws. If a man wilfully puts his hand into the fire, it will be burned;

if he sins, he will ultimately suffer for it; if he shuts his mental eyes to the light of God's truth, he will not see it.

The power of God, especially in regard to predestination, being brought out into such strong prominence in the Koran, it is not surprising that fear and passive resignation, rather than love and active devotion, appear to be the prevailing attitude of the Mohammedan mind towards Him. This is indicated by the very name of their religion, 'Islam or 'resignation to the will of God;' and by the designation of the faithful as 'Mussulman' or 'Moslem,' 'the resigned.' It was the aim of the founder of the sect of the Wahabees in the last century to restore the faith of Mahomet in its purity and integrity, as taught in the Koran. The absolute power of the Deity is expressed by the Wahabees in the simple formula 'La Ilah illa Allah.' The words themselves seem harmless and true: literally rendered, they merely signify 'There is no God but one God;' but their full import, we are assured, amounts to a great deal more. It amounts to a declaration that this one Supreme Being is 'the only force in the world, and that all things else, matter or spirit, instinct or intelligence, physical or moral, are nothing but pure, unconditional passiveness, alike in movement or in quiescence, in action or in capacity."[1] Such is the God of the sect which prides itself on having revived the teaching of the Koran in its utmost purity. Such, then, is the God of the Koran, the God whom we are there taught to believe was the God whom Abraham worshipped in spirit and in truth, of whom the true knowledge had been lost, which it was the mission of Mahomet to restore. Whether the God of Abraham is more fully and faithfully presented to us in the pages of the Koran or in the pages of the Bible, I leave the readers of these passages which I have contrasted, and others like them, to decide. Had Mahomet really known the Bible, it seems almost incredible that he should have imagined himself the depositary of a new and special revelation

[1] W. G. Palgrave, 'Central Arabia,' vol. i., p. 365, cc. viii.

concerning the attributes of the Divine Being; for all, and more than all, which he affects to disclose was to be found already revealed in the Books of Genesis, of Job, and of the Psalms alone. The intervention of the Angel Gabriel would have been a superfluous waste of divine power. But it appears to be very doubtful whether Mahomet could read; and, if he could, yet more doubtful whether he ever perused the canonical books of the Old and New Testaments.

He may have read, or heard read, portions of the Prophets or the Psalms, which may have suggested some of the grander passages in the Koran about the attributes of the Deity; but, on the other hand, all his knowledge of Biblical incidents and characters seems not derived from the sacred history itself, but culled from a variety of sources, the Talmud, the Targum, and the Midrash of the Jews, the spurious Gospels of the Christians, and Arabian and Syrian tradition, ranging from the beautiful and probable down to the puerile and grotesque.

The history of the most prominent characters of the Old Testament is either totally disfigured in the Koran, or supplemented with long circumstantial stories, which for the most part destroy the consistency and personality of the character. Some of the tales, for instance, related about Abraham are beautiful and instructive, and in harmony with what we read elsewhere about the patriarch, though they may not be actually true; but others are so silly that no sound critic could possibly admit the incidents of both as real occurrences in the life of the same person.

As a specimen of the higher kind, take the following account, borrowed from the Talmud, of the conversion of Abraham from the idolatry of his countrymen: 'When the night overshadowed him, he saw a star, and he said, "This is my Lord;" but when it set he said, "I like not gods which set." And when he saw the moon rising he said, "This is my Lord;" but when he saw it set he said, "Verily, if my Lord direct me not, I shall become one of those who go astray." And when he saw the sun rising he said, "This is my Lord, this is the greatest;" but when it set he said, "O, my people, verily I am clean of that which ye associate with God: I direct my face unto Him Who has created the Heavens and the earth. I am of the right faith, and am not one of the idolaters."' We may fairly believe that we have here, though cast into that vivid dramatic form which legend commonly assumes, the record of a true fact: the gradual elevation of the patriarch's mind from the superstitious worship of the heavenly bodies prevalent among his countrymen, to a purer and more spiritual faith. The accounts, on the other hand, of his destruction of the images of ancestral deities, and of the attempt of Nimrod to put him to death by burning, are too foolish to be looked upon as anything but purely mythical. The life of Moses is not so much distorted as the lives of some other characters, Solomon, for instance, who is turned into a kind of wonder-working magician; but the narrative of the Exodus, and of the settlement in Canaan, is overlaid with such a mass of tedious legendary rubbish, that the mind of the reader becomes fatigued and bewildered, and thankfully escapes from the fantastic shadows of Fairyland into the serene daylight of real history. Viewing the Koran, therefore, as a compilation, the critical, artistic power of the compiler cannot be ranked high.

It is needless to say that the idea of a plurality of persons in one Godhead was utterly repugnant to the rigid monotheism taught by Mahomet. His vague acquaintance with Christianity seems to have led him into supposing that Christians acknowledged, and even in some degree worshipped, what he calls 'companions' of God, and taught that sons and daughters were born to him. This strange misconception seems to have arisen partly from confused information about the doctrine of the Holy Trinity, which he seems actually to have thought involved the worship of God the Father, Jesus, and the Virgin Mary as co-ordinate deities; partly perhaps from the tendency to saint-worship, which was beginning to grow up in the Church.

The foundation, therefore, of the Christian creed, the divine Sonship and incarnation of our blessed Lord, was emphatically denied and denounced by the apostle of Islam. It is doubtful indeed if the Christian doctrine was ever fairly and reasonably put before him, the Christianity with which he came in contact being probably tainted with Manicheism, Nestorianism, and other common forms of Oriental error; but at any rate he conceived it to be a part of his mission as a preacher of pure monotheism to declare that Jesus was not God, and that divine honours ought not to be paid to Him. Mahomet's aim was to show that the life and character of Jesus had been totally misunderstood and misrepresented: that He had really come only as a prophet, only to begin the work which Mahomet himself was destined to complete: namely, the restoration to its original purity of the monotheistic faith of Abraham; a design which the believers in Jesus had frustrated by unduly exalting Him to the level of the Deity.

Against the Jews he maintained that Jesus was, like himself, an inspired prophet and reformer; against the Christians that He was not more than this. Hence the peculiar aversion of Jew and Christian alike from the religion of Islam. Each was irritated by the assumption of superiority on the part of this rival to both, which required the Jew to believe more, and the Christian to believe less, than was contained in the creed of his forefathers. According to the teaching of the Koran, the Jews would be condemned because they rejected Christ as a prophet, the Christians because they adored Him as the Son of God.

The intolerant tone, however, of the Koran towards Judaism and Christianity increases very much with the gradual growth of Mahomet's power, and the extension of his views of conquest. At first the language is mild, almost conciliatory, and, as concerning the ultimate condition of the Christian, hopeful: take the following as a specimen; 'Surely those who believe and those who Judaise, and Christians and Sabæans, whoever believeth in God and the last day, and doeth that which is right, shall have their reward with their Lord: there shall come no fear on them, neither shall they be grieved.' And yet more strongly: 'Unto every one of you were given a law and an open path, and if God had pleased, He had surely made you one people; but He hath thought fit to give you different laws that He might try you in that which He hath given you respectively. Therefore strive to equal each other in good works. Unto God shall ye all return, and then will He declare unto you that concerning which ye have disagreed.' But as time goes on, this mild language is exchanged for stern, uncompromising denunciation alike of Christian and Jew; and as the rule laid down in the Koran itself is that where passages are discordant, the later revelation abrogates the earlier, the moderate passages just cited must go for nothing.

The references in the Koran to the life of our Lord exhibit a wider and wilder departure from sober history than the references to characters of the Old Testament. In the pages of the Koran the life of Jesus is dressed up with those fantastic and puerile stories of unnecessary and unseemly wonders with which the Apocryphal Gospels abound, and which rob the character of that divine dignity and simplicity which in the genuine Gospels excite our admiration and our love. The events connected with the birth of John the Baptist are related in tolerable harmony with the Gospel narrative. Not so those which concern the birth and infancy of our blessed Lord. In the Koran the Angel Gabriel not only announces the future birth of Christ to the Virgin Mary, but the conception of the Divine Son is represented as due to his influence. The birth of Jesus is described as having taken place under a palm-tree in the desert, whither his mother had wandered. Being nearly exhausted from want of food and drink, she is directed by Gabriel to shake the branches of the tree, whereupon ripe dates immediately fall from them, and a spring of pure water gushes forth from its roots. She takes the child home, who speaks in his cradle, and announces himself as a prophet of God. When older he animates a bird made of clay, to convince his companions of his prophetical destiny; but it is expressly said that this and other miracles were wrought by the permission of God, not by his own power. Some hazy account of the Holy Eucharist which had been brought to Mahomet may perhaps have given birth to the curious statement in the Koran, that, at the request of Jesus, God caused a table laden with provisions to descend from heaven, that the day of its descent might become a festival day to his disciples. The reality of the crucifixion is explained away by the adoption of the common Gnostic theory that God frustrated the design of the Jews by taking up the real Jesus into heaven, while His enemies wasted their rage upon a phantom substituted for Him. As a consequence of this view, the resurrection disappears altogether as part of the history of our Lord and faith in the resurrection of all men, although an integral part of the Mohammedan creed, is not based in the Koran on the fact of a risen Christ, but on the power of an Almighty Creator to renew and revive that which He originally made. The miracle of *re*-creation, it is remarked, is not greater than the miracle of creation.

Of any notion of the Holy Spirit, not merely as a Person, but even as a direct influence or energy from the Deity operating on man, I cannot find any trace in the Koran. The cold, rigid monotheism which Mahomet taught, did not tolerate the idea of such close personal communion between man and his Maker. The interpretation put upon the promise of the Paraclete in St. John xvi. is the most curious instance either of astounding ignorance or of audacious imposture, to be found in the whole of the Koran. First, παράκλητος is confounded with περικλυτός, which signifies 'renowned,' or 'praised;' and then this being also the meaning of Ahmed, of which the name Mohammed is compounded, the passage is wrested into a prophecy of the coming of Mahomet.

'Jesus, the son of Mary, said, O children of Israel, verily I am the Apostle of God sent unto you confirming the law which was given before me, and bringing good tidings of an Apostle who shall come after me, whose name shall be Ahmed.' There are some other passages more dimly alluded to which Mahomet or his disciples conceived to be prophetic of himself, and he asserted that the Bible had contained more, but had been mutilated by Jews and Christians.

While, however, the Koran jealously guards the unity of the Godhead, it inculcates a belief in intermediate beings, angels and genii, who are allowed to exercise a very powerful influence upon human beings. The angels are represented in the Koran as incorporeal beings created of fire, the guardians of the throne of God, the messengers of His will between heaven and earth. At the creation of man, they were bidden to worship Adam as the son of God. All obeyed excepting the devil Eblis, who was too proud and envious to fall down before a creature of clay, and became thenceforth the enemy of man. Further, the good angels are described as impeccable and immortal, of various orders and ranks, which are distinguished by the number of their wings. To each man is assigned his guardian angel; and two who attend him, one on either side, take an account of his actions good and bad which will be produced on the day of judgment. Angels take the souls of men from their bodies; angels will summon men to judgment by the sound of the trumpet; angels intercede with God for the penitent; angels will convey the faithful to heaven, the lost to hell, where they keep guard over the fallen spirits.

The genii of the Koran are almost identical with the dæmons of the Talmud. They have more in common with angels than men, yet are inferior in several respects. Like angels, they are made of fire, they have wings, they roam up and down the world, they know future events; but they have some human qualities, they eat and drink, they are liable to human passions, and to death.

Such is Islam, viewed as a theological system—a vast advance upon polytheism, fetichism, gross and grovelling superstition of any kind; but how immeasurably below even the Jewish revelation of the nature of God, and of the relation between God and man! It is austere, comfortless, and cold. The Deity is represented not indeed as a mere philosophical abstraction, but yet as a Being, remote, unapproachable in majesty and might, wielding at His arbitrary will the destinies and movements of men, yet far aloof from them; a ruler of overwhelming power, rather than a loving and merciful, though almighty Father. There is nothing to fill up or bridge over the chasm which divides this tremendous Being from man; no divine Mediator, no quickening illuminating Spirit; for the action of angels is too precarious and vague to fulfil these offices. Islam—resignation to the irresistible will and decrees of God—expresses very well the relation between man and his Maker as set forth in the Koran; the submission of obedient fear to a power, not the devotion of love to a person. The theology, therefore, of the Koran fails to meet the profoundest religious needs of man; it removes the Creator to an immeasurable distance from the creatures whom He has made, and in the renunciation of all idea of mediation it falls infinitely below not Judaism only but Magianism and Brahmanism, which in other respects it excels. All that is good and true in the Koran concerning the nature of God, and worthy of the subject, is to be found in the Bible, if it be not borrowed from the Bible; all that is original is good for nothing, if indeed there be anything purely original, for probably most of the wilder statements could be traced to traditional sources. The genius, indeed, of Mahomet as the founder of a theological system consisted, not so much in inventing or devising anything actually new, as in piecing together fragments of other creeds, and by his commanding personal influence, tact, enthusiasm, and self-confidence, imposing this patchwork system successfully on so large a number of his fellow-countrymen. In itself, the Koran is a clumsy production. To suppose that an angel was sent from heaven to reveal the truths which it contains, would be unnecessary, for those truths are to be found more amply, more beautifully expressed elsewhere; to suppose that Gabriel was sent from heaven to reveal the childish absurdities which it contains, would be an insult to the character and work of angels.

It remains to consider briefly the teaching of the Koran concerning a future state. It may truly be said that if the lofty, though cold, conception of the Deity be the highest point in the teaching of Islam, its doctrine of a future state stands on the lowest level. It is, indeed, not raised much above the belief which has prevailed among many heathen nations. As the wild Indian imagines that the joy of the future life will consist in ranging over well stocked hunting grounds with the bow and the dog, which have been his companions in the chase on earth; as our Teutonic forefathers, ere their conversion to Christianity, looked forward to banquets in the drinking halls of Odin, as the height of celestial bliss; so did the Arab, instructed by the Koran, anticipate that the joys of Paradise would be of that sensuous and voluptuous nature which to his temperament were most alluring. 'Verdant gardens watered by clear and unfailing streams, rivers of milk the taste whereof changed not, rivers of wine pleasant to them that drink, rivers of clarified honey, perpetual shade from trees ever laden with the most delicious fruits;' these are the things which make up the scenery of the Mohammedan Paradise. Here the faithful, arrayed in costly raiment of silk, and adorned with bracelets of gold and pearls, should repose on soft couches, attended by dark eyed damsels of immortal youthfulness and superhuman beauty. Life in Paradise, in short, is made up of the most earthly sensual enjoyments, only magnified and intensified to a degree never experienced on earth, and which if they ever could be experienced, must soon cloy the appetite of the most insatiable Arab that ever lived. Of God there is no mention in these descriptions, nor, indeed, is it easy to see how the Divine Being could with decency be introduced into them. There are indeed, occasional hints of a beatific vision of the Deity to be enjoyed by the holiest of the faithful, but they are rare and dim compared with the frequent and glowing pictures of more material and corporeal delights. The pains of hell are, in their grossness, a fitting counterpart to the pleasures of Paradise. One quotation will suffice: 'They who believe not shall have garments of fire fitted to them; boiling water shall be poured upon their heads; their bowels and also their skins shall be dissolved thereby, and they shall be beaten with maces of iron. So often as they shall endeavour to get out of hell because of the anguish of their torments, they shall be dragged back into the same, and their tormentors shall say unto them, taste ye the pain of burning.'

In the description of the resurrection, and of the day of judgment, some of the Scriptural doctrine is reproduced; the archangel's trumpet, the darkening of the sun, the shaking of the earth, the reeling of the mountains, the shrivelling together of the heavens like a parched scroll; but all these are strangely jumbled with the wildest and most fantastical imaginations.

In all these descriptions of the resurrection, the judgment, and the future life, in addition to their intrinsic materiality and coarseness, we see the culminating example of a weakness which pervades the whole of the Koran, and perhaps more than anything else betrays its human origin. I mean the attempt to bring down the most inscrutable mysteries to the level of the human understanding. The minute circumstantial descriptions of holy places where angels would fear to tread, and of holy places before whom they would veil their faces, savours of a thoroughly human curiosity which imagines or invents where it cannot discover. They are in direct contradiction to the teaching of Holy Scripture, 'eye hath not seen, nor ear heard, neither hath entered into the heart of man to conceive the things which God hath prepared for them that love Him.' The reticence and reserve of the Bible concerning many subjects which most excite human curiosity is surely of some value in evidence that the origin of the sacred volume is not human, but divine. With that partial knowledge of the future state which the Gospel vouchsafes to us, the wise Christian is content. To know that 'God hath prepared for them that love Him such good things as pass man's understanding;' to know that though there be a veil between us and the other world, and 'that it doth not yet appear what we shall be,' yet if 'we purify ourselves even as Christ is pure, we shall be like Him, for we shall see Him as He is;' to know that the body of our humiliation, the body of this present fallen nature, liable to sin, to disease to death, shall be changed so as to be fashioned according to the body of Christ's glorified state; such knowledge, surely, is enough to be thankful for, enough to live by. Such knowledge is a revelation of truths which we could not have certainly discovered for ourselves, a revelation which discloses light sufficient to guide and cheer us as we plod along the dark and slippery ways of this world's night, while the greater light, which would now only dazzle and bewilder, is held back until the day comes, when the shadows shall flee away and we shall 'know even as we are known.'

LECTURE III.

MORAL TEACHING OF THE BIBLE AND THE KORAN CONTRASTED.

'Allahu Akbar! Prayer is better than sleep! O Thou bountiful One, Thy mercy ceases not! My sins are great: greater is thy mercy! I extol His perfection! Allahu Akbar.' —*The Mohammedan Call to Prayer.*

THE apostolic mission of Mahomet having been once acknowledged, it was natural that he should undertake the regulation, not only of the creed but also of the moral practice and ceremonial worship of his countrymen. The Koran consequently became the ethical digest, the civil code, the ceremonial handbook, as well as the theological oracle of his disciples. And it is obvious that if Mahomet's aim was to remodel the national life, the most effectual way of attaining it, his prophetic authority once established, was to frame a number of positive precepts touching every department of moral conduct. A peculiar character is by this method quickly but forcibly stamped upon the recipients. They become 'new creatures,' with new motives, and new purposes. They are capable of being conducted by their ruler to definite ends, because their movements are under control, because the people are more like a disciplined army, than are a people to whom greater freedom of thought and action is allowed. Nothing less than the imposition of a minute code of rules for practical life could have enabled Benedict, or Francis of Assissi, or Dominic, or Ignatius Loyola to fix such a distinct and lasting character upon the great religious orders which they created.

It was by their subjection to a system of positive precepts, moulding and regulating every department of life, that the Israelites, after their emancipation from Egypt, were trained for that peculiar position among the nations of the world which it was God's purpose to give them. Their long servitude in Egypt had crushed their spirit of independence and self-respect, had lowered their moral standard, and corrupted the pure faith of their forefathers. Nothing less than a stringent minute set of practical laws could have transformed them from a rabble of abject and superstitious slaves into a brave, God-fearing, God-loving host of free men. Such a code was given to them in the hands of their mediator, Moses; it became to them, what the Koran has become to the Mussulman, the theological, moral, ceremonial, and civil code, all in one; it taught them what to believe, how to worship, how to live. Having been converted, under the influence of their heaven-sent law, into a valorous and puissant people, they took forcible possession of the land of Canaan; and the promise made ages before to their ancestors Abraham, Isaac, and Jacob, was at last fulfilled.

Thus far there certainly seems some analogy between the effects of the law given to the Jews from God, as they believed, through Moses, and the effects of the law given to the Arabs from God, as they no less believed, through Mahomet. The aim of Mahomet was to revive among his countrymen the Arabs, as Moses revived among his countrymen the Jews, the pure faith of their common forefather Abraham. In this he succeeded to a very great extent. For a confused heap of idolatrous superstitions he substituted a pure monotheistic faith he abolished some of the most vicious practices of his countrymen, modified others; he generally raised the moral standard, improved the social condition of the people, and introduced a sober and rational ceremonial in worship. Finally he welded by this means a number of wild independent tribes, mere floating atoms, into a compact body politic, as well prepared and as eager to subdue the kingdoms of the world to their rule and to their faith, as ever the Israelites had been to conquer the land of Canaan.

But the danger of a precise system of

positive precepts regulating in minute detail the ceremonial of worship, and the moral and social relations of life, is that it should retain too tight a grip upon men when the circumstances which justified it have changed or vanished away; that the movements as it were of full-grown men should be impeded and cramped by garments fitted only for children; or to speak more correctly, perhaps, that the moral growth of those who live under such a minute system of restraints should be stunted and retarded. Amongst the Jews there was a provision made against this danger. It was one peculiar part of the mission of the Prophets to counteract that tendency to narrowness, formality, and hardness, which was the consequence of living under a rigid system of positive precepts. They kindled the spirit of worship and of morality, as opposed to the letter; they prepared the way for the purer, loftier, more free dispensation of the Gospel. The earlier system of exact and positive laws had been necessary, first to transform the character of the people, and then to maintain it; first to mark them off from all other nations as God's chosen, peculiar possession, and then to fence them round and preserve their creed and morals intact, and undefiled by the mass of heathenism which surrounded them. But lest they should confound virtue as identical with obedience to the outward requirements of the law, the voices of the Prophets were ever and anon lifted up to declare that a strict conformity to practical precepts, whether of conduct or ceremonial, would not extenuate, but rather increase, in the eyes of God the guilt of an unpurified heart and an unholy life.

To what purpose is the multitude of your sacrifices unto me? Bring no more vain oblations; incense is an abomination unto me; the new moons and sabbaths, the calling of assemblies, I cannot away with: it is iniquity, even the solemn meeting. . . . . Wash you, make you clean; put away the evil of your doings from before mine eyes; cease to do evil, learn to do well; seek judgment, relieve the oppressed, judge the fatherless, plead for the widow.' It would be unnecessary to multiply citations of similar passages, which are familiar to us all. They are all anticipations of the moral teaching of Him who pronounced woe on those hypocrites that paid tithe of mint, anise, and cummin, but omitted the weightier matters of the law, judgment, mercy, and faith.

It is obvious to any reader of the Koran that it does not contain, except perhaps in a few stray passages, any teachings analogous to the moral teaching of the Hebrew Prophets which might act as a corrective to the cramping and hardening influence of its positive precepts. Nor has any school of teachers arisen in Islam who have made it their aim to accomplish this salutary object. There have been Scribes (and probably Pharisees) in abundance, but no Prophets.

In the reformation which Mahomet effected among the Arabs, by persuading them to adopt as of divine institution a set of theological doctrines and moral precepts, it has been admitted that there seems some analogy to the reformation effected among the Israelites by Moses. It has often been considered that in the propagation of the creed of Mahomet by the sword, there is a further parallel to the forcible occupation of the land of Canaan by the Jews. There are critics who will compare the extermination or subjugation of the inhabitants of conquered territory alike by Mahomet and Joshua, and maintain that it is equally difficult to reconcile either with sound principles of morality. The supposed analogy, however, breaks down upon examination, and the case turns out to be one, not for comparison, but contrast. In the Koran, the Mussulman is absolutely and positively commanded to make war upon all those who decline to acknowledge the prophet until they submit, or, in the case of Jews and Christians, purchase exemption from conformity by the payment of tribute. The mission of the Mussulman, as declared in the Koran, is distinctly aggressive. We might say that Mahomet bequeathed to his disciples a roving commission to propagate his faith by the employment of force where persuasion failed. 'O prophet, fight for the religion of God'—'Stir up the faithful to war,' such are commands which Mahomet believed to be given him by God. 'Fight against them who believe not in God nor the last day,' 'attack the idolatrous in all the months,' such are his own exhortations to his disciples.

We need hardly stop to point out that such a charge is diametrically opposite to the commission of Christ to His Apostles, who were commanded to preach the Gospel to every creature, but were expressly forbidden to support their preaching by carnal weapons. It is more important to show that the Jews had no roving commission to go about the world making proselytes, and presenting the alternatives of tribute or the sword to such as would not accept their creed. They were commanded to take possession of only a narrow strip of land, promised ages before to their ancestors, to extirpate the inhabitants on account of their singular wickedness, and then to keep themselves aloof from their neighbours in order that the light of a pure monotheistic faith might be maintained burning undimmed amidst the darkness of surrounding heathenism. Again and again the people are reminded that the land is given them as a step towards the fulfilment of the promise made by God to their forefathers, that through their seed all nations of the earth should in the ages to come be blessed; again and again they are instructed that in destroying or expelling the inhabitants they were only instruments used for the removal of wickedness instead of some inanimate force, such as earthquake, or plague, or the fire which consumed Sodom and Gomorrah. 'Understand this day that the Lord thy God is He which goeth over before thee; as a consuming fire shall He destroy them, and bring them down before thy face. . . . . Speak not thou in thine heart after that the Lord thy God hath cast them out from before thee, saying, for my righteousness the Lord hath brought me in to possess this land. . . . . Not for thy righteousness or for the uprightness of thine heart dost thou go to possess their land; *but for the wickedness of these nations the Lord thy God doth drive them out from before thee, and that He may perform the word which the Lord sware unto thy fathers, Abraham, Isaac, and Jacob*' (Deut. ix. 3-5). The two purposes for which the Jews were permitted to take forcible possession of Canaan are here distinctly stated: the immediate purpose was the expulsion of wickedness; the ultimate far reaching purpose was, retrospectively, the fulfilment of the promise made to their forefathers; prospectively, as a part or consequence of this fulfilment, the bestowal of a blessing on all families of the earth. Meanwhile the Jews, having been once established in their country, were to abstain from aggression upon surrounding nations, and as far as possible from intercourse with them. They were to act on the defensive, to keep themselves separate and undefiled; not to compel others to accept their faith, but to wait patiently God's own time, and God's own way of extending it. In the Book of Deuteronomy (xvii.) there are some principles laid down for regulating the character and conduct of kings who might in future be appointed. They all aim at repressing the acquisition of military power, the display of military pomp, the indulgence in luxury, and the accumulation of riches to which the Oriental despots of the world were addicted. The Jewish king was not to multiply horses to himself, or wives or silver and gold. The career of Solomon was in direct disobedience to these commands, and initiated a disastrous policy of worldly greatness and ambition in his successors, which ended in the overthrow of the Empire. In the Koran, on the other hand, there is no such condemnation of these elements of earthly luxury and ostentation, and the later caliphs certainly indulged in them to their hearts' content.

The latitude of toleration allowed to the Jews towards nations alien in creed or birth, or both, was as great as possible compatibly with the necessity of keeping the chosen nation free from contamination; and much greater than many from a superficial view of the Jewish position are apt to imagine. 'Thou shalt not abhor an Edomite, for he is thy brother; thou shalt not abhor an Egyptian, because thou wast a stranger in his land.' Edomite or Egyptian children of the third generation were to be admitted as members of the congregation (Deut. xxiii. 7, 8). The league of peace made with the Gibeonites was to be observed forever, notwithstanding they had obtained it by a fraudulent artifice. This scrupulous adherence to a pledge once given, this 'swearing to a neighbour, and disappointing him not, though it were to their own hindrance,' presents a striking contrast to the acts of treachery which were not only connived at by Mahomet, but in some cases expressly sanctioned.

Nothing, again, is more continually and solemnly reiterated in the pages of the Pentateuch than the duty of showing kindness to strangers. The command is always based upon a touching appeal to the recollection of their own former condition as strangers and sojourners in Egypt. 'Thou shalt not oppress a stranger, for ye know the heart of a stranger, seeing ye were strangers in the land of Egypt.' 'Thou shalt neither vex a stranger nor oppress him, seeing ye were strangers in the land of Egypt.' The Koran also enjoins repeatedly and in very emphatic language the duty of showing kindness to the stranger and the orphan, and of treating slaves, if converted to the faith, with the consideration and respect due to believers. The duty even of mercy to the lower animals is not forgotten, and it is to be thankfully acknowledged that Mohammedanism as well as Buddhism shares with Christianity the honour of having given birth to Hospitals and Asylums for the insane and sick. But ardent admirers of Islam are so much captivated by these laudable traits that they sometimes unduly magnify them, and underrate the teachings of the Bible in reference to the same subjects. To take the case of slavery, for instance; persons filled with admiration of the humane treatment of the slave inculcated in the Koran, and as a rule practised in Mohammedan countries, are apt to forget that slavery after all is distinctly recognized by the Koran as an integral part of the social system; that the Mohammedan slave could not look forward like the Hebrew to his release in the seventh year; and that, while the Koran enjoins kindness in general terms, there are not such often repeated and touching warnings as we find in the Pentateuch against oppression of slaves and hired servants, not such distinct and minute provisions for their happiness and welfare. 'Thou shalt not oppress an hired servant that is poor and needy, whether he be of thy brethren or of thy strangers that are in thy land within thy gates: at his day thou shalt give him his hire, neither shall the sun go down upon it, for he is poor and setteth his heart upon it . . . . thou shalt remember that thou wast a bondman in Egypt, and the Lord thy God redeemed thee thence.' If a master struck a slave so as to cause the loss of an eye or a tooth, the slave was to go free for his eye's sake, or his tooth's sake; if he caused his death, the master was to be punished. When the slave was released in the seventh year, his wife and children accompanied him unless the wife had been given him by his master. In that case, and in that case only, the master could retain her (Exod. xxi.[1]) The runaway slave was not to be restored to his master. 'Thou shalt not deliver unto his master the servant which is escaped from his master unto thee: he shall dwell with thee in that place which he shall choose in one of thy gates where it liketh him best: thou shalt not oppress him' (Deut. xxiii. 15).

By such like enactments did the law of Moses mitigate the condition of slavery. The Gospel has done more. It did not violently interfere with any of the existing social or political institutions amongst which it arose; it accepted them, it made the best of them. It did not preach rebellion against the slave-

[1] Mr. Bosworth Smith's references to the Pentateuch on this subject are defective and one-sided 'Lectures on Mohammedanism,' (p. 245.)

owner, or the despot; but it was ever slowly yet surely sapping the despotism alike of the slave-owner and the political tyrant at its roots by proclaiming principles of justice and mercy, and infusing a spirit of brotherhood, which were inconsistent with oppression in any form. The conduct of St. Paul towards the slave Onesimus and his master Philemon is a typical illustration of the general attitude of Christianity towards the institution of slavery as a whole. He sends back the fugitive, but requests Philemon that he may be received, not *as* a slave, but as a *brother beloved;* because like the master he had become a Christian, was a member of the same spiritual family, an inheritor of the same Heavenly kingdom (Philem. 16).

To pass from the treatment of slaves to the treatment of enemies, 'Islam, tribute, or the sword,' is the well-known formula which sums up the teaching of the Koran concerning this matter. 'When ye encounter the unbelievers, strike off their heads until ye have made a great slaughter among them; and bind them in bonds, and either give them a free dismission afterwards or exact a ransom until the war shall have laid down its arms.' This is mild compared with many other passages where the alternative of release is not suggested. The Israelites, as was observed just now, were to abstain from aggression, except upon the inhabitants of that land in which they were to act as God's instruments for the extirpation of wickedness. The capture of towns in Canaan, therefore, but in Canaan only, was to be followed by complete destruction of all that breathed therein. If forced into war with more distant countries, when the Jewish army came before a city peace was to be proclaimed. If this was not accepted and the city was besieged and captured, the men only were to be put to the sword; the women and children were to be saved alive (Deut. xx.). Under the Mosaic law women taken captive in war were not to be degraded to the condition of slave concubines. If a man wished to make one his wife, she had first to go through a kind of religious ceremonial of purification, and then she was allowed a month of mourning for her old home before she was married. If the husband afterwards wished to put her away, she was free to go wherever she pleased; the man was not to sell her or in any way to make merchandise of her (Deut. xxi.). These provisions for the honor of female captives form a striking contrast to the law of the Koran, which, while it endeavours to alleviate the evils of polygamy by restricting the number of a man's wives to four, places no limit whatever to the number of his concubines, and makes no provision for the mitigation of their unhappy lot.

Of course we do not forget that the regulations of the Pentateuch concerning war were frequently violated, like many other particulars of the moral law; yet the deeds of the most merciless kings of Israel and Judah will hardly offer a parallel to one act of barbarous cruelty approved, if not actually ordered, by Mahomet. Omm Kirfa, an aged woman, chieftainess of a tribe which had molested and plundered the caravans of the faithful, having been made captive, was tied by the legs to two camels, which were then driven in opposite directions, so that her body was literally torn asunder. I am not aware that the exploits even of modern Bashi Bazouks and Circassians can rival such an 'atrocity' as this, committed under the sanction of the founder of Islam. If it be scornfully observed that things as horrible have been done by men bearing the name of Christians, and sometimes professedly in the name of Christianity, we of course admit what every Christian with shame and sorrow must confess. Only such alleged parallels prove nothing. The 'tu quoque' argument is always a poor one, and in this instance it is peculiarly unfortunate. Wars undertaken in the name of religion by Christians are in direct disobedience both to the spirit and letter of the Gospel; whereas religious wars undertaken by Mohammedans are in conformity with the practice and precept of the founder of their religion. Christianity, therefore, cannot be made in any way chargeable with cruelties committed in wars which are themselves in contravention of the command of Christ. That men have (sometimes with a sincere zeal for God only not according to knowledge) attempted to propagate the Christian faith by war with its concomitant horrors in direct *disobedience* to the command of Christ, does not improve the position of the Mussulman when he propagates his creed by war in direct *obedience* to the command of Mahomet.

One more illustration may suffice to close the contrast between the Pentateuch and the Koran respecting the conduct of war. In the book of Deuteronomy the destruction of such trees in an enemy's country as bore edible fruit is expressly forbidden: 'Thou shalt not cut them down to employ them in the siege, for the tree of the field is man's life.' On one occasion when some palm trees (one of the principal sources of food to the Arab) were an impediment to some military operation of the prophet, he produced a special revelation authorizing their removal. 'What palm trees ye cut down or left standing were so cut down or left standing by the will of God, that He might disgrace the evil doers.'

The vices most prevalent in Arabia in the time of Mahomet which are most sternly denounced and absolutely forbidden in the Koran were drunkenness, unlimited concubinage and polygamy, the destruction of female infants, reckless gambling, extortionate usury, superstitious arts of divination and magic. The abolition of some of these evil customs, and the mitigation of others, was a gread advance in the morality of the Arabs, and is a wonderful and honourable testimony to the zeal and influence of the reformer. The total suppression of female infanticide and of drunkenness is the most signal triumph of his work; yet it may be observed that the excesses of cruelty and licentiousness of which Mohammedans can be guilty, notwithstanding abstinence from wine, proves that total abstinence from one evil thing is not in itself so good a security for virtue as the Christian principle of soberness and temperance in all things.

The condition of women in Arabia seems to have been improved in three ways by the provisions of the Koran. The transmission of a man's wives to his heir as part of his property, like his furniture or any other household chattel, was forbidden. The right of a woman to a share in her father's or husband's property was declared, and, as already stated, the legal number of wives for any one man was limited to four. Mahomet himself was exempted from this restriction by a special revelation in his favour. Under the Jewish law, polygamy was tolerated; but it was not distinctly sanctioned, as it is in the Koran, by the definition of a fixed allowable number of wives, and therefore no impediment was placed in the way of the ultimate removal of the system by the gradual growth of purer and truer views respecting the married state and the position of women in society.

The laws respecting divorce in the Koran are vile, and reveal the condition of the wife as suffering under the extreme degradation and servitude common in all Oriental countries. The husband might put away his wife and take her back again at pleasure; but if divorce had been thrice repeated she could not return to her husband except on one revolting condition, that she should first be married to another man and live with him for one whole day and night. We read of one follower of the prophet who had offspring by sixteen wives. As he could not have possessed more than four at any one time, his case is a remarkable illustration of the facility of divorce. With these abominable customs contrast the command in Deuteronomy (xxiv. 4), which expressly forbids a man to take back a wife who has been once divorced and married to another. In Deuteronomy, again (xxi.), we find a law directed against the effects of that favouritism and jealousy which are among the many banes and curses of polygamy. 'If a man have two wives, one beloved and the other hated, and they have borne him children, both the beloved and hated, and if the first born son be hers that was hated; then it shall be when he maketh his sons to inherit that which he hath, that he may not make the son of the beloved first born before the son of the hated, but he shall acknowledge the son of the hated for the first born by giving him a double portion of all that he hath: the right of the first born is his.'

The exhortations to almsgiving as a solemn duty commanded by God and owed to man are, as is well known, very numerous in the Koran. It is perhaps the point on which the teaching of the Koran may most fairly be compared with the teaching of the Pentateuch, yet there are not such careful and particular instructions in the Koran as in the Pentateuch for ministering to the necessities of the 'stranger, the fatherless, and the widow.' The certainty of a rich reward in the life to come to those who bestow alms is promised in the Koran in terms which sound rather like a bribe to benevolence, and which might not improbably foster pride in the almsgiver. Future punishment is predicted with equal positiveness on those who should neglect the duty. 'Unto such as believe and bestow alms shall be given a great reward,' but he who did not pay his legal contribution of alms would have a serpent twisted about his neck on the day of resurrection.

The duties of prayer and fasting are inculcated in the Koran as co-ordinate with the duty of almsgiving; and the punctual and scrupulous observance by the Mussulman of the appointed hours of prayer, and the appointed season of fasting, is notorious and edifying. According to the traditional account of Mahomet's nocturnal journey to the seventh Heaven, he was commanded by the Almighty to impose on his disciples the obligation of saying prayers fifty times a day. By the advice of Moses, he supplicated and obtained a mitigation of this intolerable burden, and the number was gradually reduced to five. The observance of these hours was indispensable. The prayers might be shortened on the march or in the camp, when some emergency demanded action without delay; but the omissions were to be made up afterwards when the pressure of danger or haste was at an end. Cleanliness was designated by Mahomet as the key of prayer, even as prayer was the gate of Paradise; and accordingly his disciples were forbidden to enter on their devotions without having washed the face, hands, and feet. In the absence or scarcity of water, the believer is by a special permission in the Koran to use sand as a substitute.

In the beginning of his career, when he was cultivating friendly relations with the Jews, Mahomet instructed his disciples to turn their faces, when they prayed, towards Jerusalem; but after all hopes of conciliating the Jews were at an end, Mecca was established as the Holy City, the centre of attraction to which the eyes and thoughts of the faithful worshipper were to be directed. The temple indeed at Mecca, the Kaaba, was considered by Mahomet, in common with the rest of his countrymen, as far exceeding Jerusalem in antiquity and sanctity as a spot consecrated to pure worship. It was supposed to be almost coeval with the world. The original having been destroyed by the deluge, the temple was rebuilt, according to Arabian tradition, by Abraham and Ishmael; but the black stone was venerated as a genuine relic of the primæval building, having been let down, it was said, by God to earth at the request of Adam, after his expulsion from Paradise. The duty of visiting this holy place is urged in the Koran with no less frequency and solemnity than the duties of almsgiving and prayer. Every Mohammedan, as he values the prospect of happiness in the life to come, is bound to make the pilgrimage once, at least, in his lifetime, and those who are able should make it every year in the appointed month. If prevented by sickness or any other pressing necessity, the omission was suffered to be redeemed by offerings and a ten days' fast.

The Koran prescribes that one month in the year, the month Ramadan, should be observed as a very strict fast. From sunrise to sunset, neither food nor drink must pass the lips, but after sunset the natural appetites may be moderately gratified. As the Arabian year is lunar, each month in the course of thirty-three years runs through all the different seasons. Consequently when the month Ramadan falls in the middle of the summer, the length of the days and the severity of the heat cause such vigorous abstinence from sunrise to sunset to be extremely mortifying.

We have now touched upon the main precepts, ethical and ceremonial, contained in the Koran. The following passage is perhaps the best summary of the moral teaching which could be picked out of the whole book, especially showing that Mahomet himself did not value ceremonial unless it was attended by that real devotion on the part of the worshipper which all ceremonial is intended to express:

'There is no piety in turning your faces towards the east or the west; but he is pious who believeth in God, and the Last Day, and the Angels and the Scriptures and the Prophets, who for the love of God dispenses his wealth to his kinsfolk, to the orphans, and to the needy, and the wayfarer, and to those who ask, and for ransoming, who observeth prayer, and payeth the legal alms, and who belongs to them that are faithful to their engagements, when they have engaged in them, and are patient under ills and hardships and in time of trouble; these are they who are just and those who fear the Lord.'

We get here a taste, a gleam, of that higher and more spiritual moral teaching which, as was pointed out at the beginning of this lecture, is the most salutary counterpoise to the stiffness and hardness of bare ethical precepts and ceremonial regulations, and to their tendency to contract men's notions of morality. Yet if all the sublime teaching of the Hebrew Prophets did not suffice to rescue the Jews from formalism, if our Lord had to denounce pretentious prayer-making, ostentatious almsgiving, superstitious ablutions, an inordinate veneration of Jerusalem and the Temple as the only spots where prayer would be acceptable, it is impossible to forbear thinking that the minute directions of the Koran concerning the times and places of prayers, and fasting, and pilgrimage, concerning the amount of almsgiving, and its consequent reward, must be perilous to the preservation of a large-minded, large-hearted piety. The tendency of the human heart to self-deceit and formalism is so strong that when men are tied down to the performance of certain religious functions, minutely and precisely fixed in respect to time and manner, so that neither less nor more is required of them, they will very commonly (though perhaps often unconsciously to themselves) fall into the error of imagining that there is a peculiar intrinsic merit and virtue in the mere discharge of those duties. Morality is viewed not in the abstract, but in the concrete, as consisting in a bundle of religious observances rather than in a certain disposition of the heart towards God and man.

Thus, in contrasting the moral teaching of the Koran with the moral teaching of the Old Testament, and still more of the New Testament, the point which cannot fail to strike the careful student is this, that it deals much more with sin and virtue in fragmentary detail than as wholes. It deals with acts more than principles, with outward practice more than inward motives, with precept and command more than exhortation. For instance, there are commands to give full measure, to weigh with a just balance, to abstain from wine and gambling, to treat certain persons with kindness; but on the graces of truth and honesty, of temperance and mercy, as principles of wide application, the Koran does not dwell. I have failed to discover a single passage which touches on the virtue of meekness properly so called. Patience is inculcated, but chiefly as a condition of success in propagating the faith of Islam; for unless the believer was patient under insult and adversity, the cause of his religion might be injured by the provocation of an attack.[1]

[1] It is, however, only fair to give a specimen, which may be a sample of many more like it, of the check which reve-

Nowhere in the Koran, as in the Bible, is sin set forth as the subtle leaven, the moral disease, pervading and corrupting human nature, as the evil principle of which all particular forms of wickedness are the outcome. The Koran prescribes the practice of certain virtues, and condemns the practice of certain vices; it encourages by promising rewards, it deters by threatening punishment; but it does not hold up before man the hatefulness and ugliness of *all* sin *as a whole.* It does not depict vividly and forcibly the sinfulness of his fallen nature and of the impossibility of his really cleansing himself in the sight of God. Of the need of propitiation for daily and inevitable transgressions, there is not a word. This places at once a

rence for the precepts of the Koran could place upon angry passions. As one of the sons of Ali, Mahomet's nephew, was dining, a slave dropped by accident a dish of scalding broth upon him. The poor creature fell prostrate before his master, and, to deprecate his rage, repeated a verse from the Koran: 'Paradise is for those who command their anger;' 'I am not angry,' was the reply. 'And for those who pardon offences;' I pardon your offence.' 'And for those who return good for evil;' 'I give you your liberty and four hundred pieces of silver.'

vast interval between the standpoint of the Mohammedan and the Jewish religions. The essence of the Biblical ethics is the insufficiency of man to fulfil the divine law of righteousness, the hopelessness of his obtaining the favour of God, or opening the gates of Heaven by the strength of his own merits. The necessity, therefore, of propitiation and atonement runs through the teaching of the Bible from beginning to end. Every offering under the Jewish Law was an acknowledgment of the offerer's inability to meet God's demands; it was a cry for mercy. All the offerings were summed up and completely discharged for man in the Life crowned by the Death of Jesus Christ; and the attitude of the Christian towards God is that of humility and hope, his moral motive is gratitude and love. The moral motive of Islam is a solemn sense of the duty of obedience and submission to an Almighty Ruler; whereas the moral motive of Christianity is love to an Almighty Father, an all-sympathising Redeemer, Brother, and Friend.

The moral teaching of the Koran, put into a few words, seems to amount to this: 'Obey these rules for moral conduct, and conform to this prescribed ceremonial in worship, because they are commanded by God and His prophet, and you will be rewarded with everlasting bliss in the life to come:[1] disobey them, and you will be rewarded with everlasting torment.' Such a system is not calculated to inspire hope in the sinner, or to foster humility in the righteous, and is, to say the least, not unlikely to gender the delusion that the whole of practical morality and piety is enclosed within the narrow compass of a fixed number of precepts. There is no foundation laid in the Koran for that far-reaching charity which, under the Gospel regards all men as equal in the sight of God, and recognises no distinctions into races and classes; there is no foundation for

[1] Not, indeed, because you deserve it. Mahomet is careful to say that future bliss is the gift of God's mercy; but yet it is as confidently asserted that this gift will follow the discharge of certain prescribed duties, as if it were the price paid for them.

that keen sense of sinfulness, unworthiness, insufficiency, for that distrust of self, and that reliance on one higher and mightier than ourselves, which has enabled all God's saints to do and to suffer things beyond their natural power, making good the saying of St. Paul, 'When I am weak, then am I strong.'

LECTURE IV.

THE PRACTICAL RESULTS OF CHRISTIANITY AND ISLAM.

By their fruits ye shall know them.'

WE have considered Islam hitherto in itself; the nature of its origin, and the character of its Founder; its Sacred Book, and the teaching theological and moral therein contained. But the best test, after all, of the truth and worth of a religion must be the practical one. What has it effected? Is mankind the better for it or the worse? What are its fruits? Men do not gather figs from thorns, neither from a bramble bush gather they grapes. Caution, however, must be observed in the application of this test. It is not always easy to trace how far the prosperity or the depression of any given country is owing to the religion which prevails there or to other causes: race, climate, foreign invasion, and the like. Nor is it the primary object of religion to secure man's happiness in this world, but to guide him in his aspirations to the world above. But it seems safe to take our stand upon this principle, which may be called the law of concomitant variations: that if prosperity has followed the establishment of a certain form of religion, increasing where it is strong, and decreasing where it is weak, and this in a multitude of instances,—that is to say, in divers countries, and in divers ages of the world,—there must be something in that religion which is conducive to prosperity; and, in like manner, that if the reverse follows, there must be something in that religion adverse to prosperity, and consequently that such religion cannot as a whole be divine. 'The light which leads astray is not the light from Heaven.'

Let us, then, briefly survey what has taken place in those countries where Islam has been planted. First of all, it must be freely granted that to his own people Mahomet was a great benefactor. He was born in a country where political organization, and rational faith, and pure morals were unknown. He introduced all three. By a single stroke of masterly genius, he simultaneously reformed the political condition, the religious creed, and the moral practice of his countrymen; in the place of many independent tribes he left a nation; for a superstitious belief in Gods many and Lords many he established a reasonable belief in one Almighty yet beneficent Being; taught men to live under an abiding sense of this Being's superintending care, to look to Him as the rewarder, and to fear Him as the punisher, of evil doers. He vigorously attacked, and modified or suppressed, many gross and revolting customs which had prevailed in Arabia down to this time. For an abandoned profligacy was substituted a carefully regulated polygamy, and the practice of destroying female infants was effectually abolished.

As Islam gradually extended its conquest beyond the boundaries of Arabia, many barbarous races whom it absorbed became in like manner participators in its benefits. The Turk, the Indian, the Negro, and the Moor, were compelled to cast away their idols, to abandon their licentious rites and customs, to turn to the worship of one God, to a decent ceremonial and an orderly way of life. The faith even of the more enlightened Persian was purified; he learned that good and evil are not co-ordinate powers, but that just and unjust are alike under the sway of one All-wise and Holy Ruler, who 'ordereth all things in heaven and earth.'

For barbarous nations, then, especially,—nations which were more or less in the condition of Arabia itself at the time of Mahomet—nations in the condition of Africa at the present day, with little or no civilization, and without a reasonable religion—Islam certainly comes as a blessing, as a turning from darkness to light, and from the power of Satan unto God. But the imposition of a system good for barbarians upon people already possessing higher forms of civilization, and the principles of a purer faith, is not a blessing, but a curse. Nay more, even the system which was good for people when they were in a barbarous state may become positively mischievous to those same people when they begin to emerge from their barbarism under its influence into a higher condition. The danger, as was remarked at the beginning of the last lecture, attaching to a system which minutely regulates every department of social life, moral conduct, and religious ceremonial, is that it should be held rigorously in force upon men when they have outgrown the need of it. It may be good as far as it goes; good relatively to certain circumstances, and perhaps, for the circumstances under which it was first devised, the best possible; but if it be not absolutely and perfectly good, good for *all* times, places, and persons, it must at some time, in certain places, and to certain persons become not a help, but a hindrance, to civilization and moral progress.

The *immediate* effect, then, of the introduction of Islam among barbarous races, is to raise them considerably in the scale of humanity. Its action in this respect is probably more speedy than the action of Christianity, owing to that definiteness, positiveness, minuteness, with which it is brought to bear on practical life, of which we have already spoken; it lays down rules and enforces conformity to them, and consequently a more immediate return is yielded in a visible reformation of manners, than is possible in the case of a religion which inculcates large principles for the due application of which much must be left to the individual conscience.

But when we turn to consider the effects of the introduction of Islam among nations already acquainted with the civilization of the Roman Empire and the light of the Christian religion, the picture is very different. We are compelled by the facts of history to decline believing that in these cases Islam, viewed as a whole, has been anything but an enormous evil. Claiming, as it did, to be the truth, the whole truth, and nothing but the truth, it tolerated no rival; Christianity and Christian civilization were voluntarily or by compulsion to bend the knee before it. The most effectual plan was to make a clean sweep of both. Let us see how far the first Mohammedan conquerors acted upon it. I will quote the words of that most eminent and trustworthy historian of the Byzantine Empire, Mr. Finlay. 'The Arab conquest,' he says, 'of Palestine and Syria, not only put an end to the political power of the Romans, which had lasted seven hundred years, but it also rooted out every trace of the Greek civilization introduced by the conquests of Alexander the Great which had flourished in the country for upwards of nine centuries.'[1]

The celebrated reply of the Caliph Omar, when asked what should be done with the library of Alexandria, illustrates the policy of the Saracens in Egypt as elsewhere. 'If,' said he, 'these writings agree with the Book

[1] Vol. i. p. 445, 2d edition.

of God, they are useless and need not be preserved; if they disagree, they are pernicious, and ought to be destroyed;' and accordingly the library was burned. Here, again, Mr. Finlay remarks, 'political sagacity convinced the Arabs that it was necessary to exterminate Greek civilization in order to destroy Greek influence. The Goths, who sought only to plunder the empire, might spare the libraries of the Greeks; but the Mohammedans, whose object was to convert or subdue, considered it a duty to root out everything that presented any obstacle to the ultimate success of their schemes for the advent of Mohammedan civilization.' Tracing their career of conquest along the northern coast of Africa, he concludes by observing: 'The Saracens were singularly successful in all their projects of destruction; in a short time, both Latin and Greek civilization was exterminated on the southern shores of the Mediterranean.'[1]

[1] Vol. i. pp. 450, 451, 2nd edition.

In Spain, after the establishment of the Caliphate of Cordova in 936 A.D., order succeeded a state of anarchy, which had been disastrous alike to the conquerors and to the conquered, and under a happy succession of vigorous, and in many instances, upright and enlightened Caliphs, commerce and agriculture, science, literature, and the arts, were carried to a higher degree of perfection than in any other country under Arabian rule. I am not just yet going to discuss the question, how far Arabic science and art were original, how far borrowed from the lower Greek Empire. What I wish to point out at present, is, that although in Spain a high order, as it seemed, of prosperity grew up, yet it was only partial, it did not extend to the whole of the population; the subject Christians were never conciliated, or assimilated; they were not happy or content; and their resistance to the Moors, as they were called, never ceased, from the day the first Moor set foot in the land until the day the last was expelled from it.

From this rapid survey of the early conquests of the Saracens, two facts seem abundantly plain: first, that the claim of Islam to supersede every other form of faith and of civilisation was so absolute, that it could not tolerate their presence side by side with itself; and that, as a consequence, it never could get a permanent hold upon any country which had become *thoroughly* leavened with the Christianity, the civilisation, and the law of the Roman Empire. It is a very inexact way of speaking to say that it 'crumpled up the empire;'[1] it would be more correct to say that it grated on the edges. Countries like Syria, Palestine, Egypt, and northern Africa, on the fringe of the empire, countries whose inhabitants were regarded as rebels by the Emperor, and as heretics by the Greek Church, fell before Islam, but on the heart of the empire it made no impression. Once it menaced Constantinople, but it was hurled back by the might and valour of Leo the Isaurian. The second fact is this; that in

[1] Bosworth Smith, Lect. i. p. 26, 2nd edition.

those countries on the skirts of the empire where it did succeed in planting itself, this was accomplished at the cost of uprooting as far as possible the religion and civilisation which it found there. To quote again from Mr. Finlay: 'Of all the native populations in the countries subdued, the Arabs of Syria alone appear to have immediately adopted the new religion of their co-national race; but the great mass of the Christians in Syria, Mesopotamia, Egypt, Cyrenaïca, and Africa, clung firmly to their faith, and the decline of Christianity in all those countries is to be attributed rather to the extermination than to the conversion of the Christian inhabitants. The decrease in the number of the Christians was invariably attended by a decrease in the number of the inhabitants, and arose from the oppressive treatment which they suffered under the Mohammedan rulers of these countries—a system of tyranny which was at last carried so far as to reduce whole provinces to unpeopled deserts.'[1]

[1] Vol. i. p. 452.

Looking now beyond the limits of the Roman Empire, the country where we might most reasonably expect Mohammedanism to have accomplished great things is Persia. There Islam had a fair field to work upon; it became the national religion; there were no infidel Europeans to resist and hinder its free development. But, as if by a strange perverseness, Islam never seems to flourish so well as when it is attacked or attacking. Left to itself unmolested it loses energy, or wastes its strength upon internal strife. In Persia it split into a multitude of contending sects, more occupied in devouring one another than in promoting the welfare of their common country. The Persian is probably the most polished, well educated, and literary, of all Mohammedans; yet his country is the most deplorable specimen of mismanagement, political, commercial, and everything else. Fertile as the country is, and scanty as is the population, there is none which has suffered more cruelly from famine; and, as a last resource, the helpless government was reduced to the ignominious necessity, a short time back, of calling in the aid of a foreigner, a European, to save the country from becoming a total wreck.

Incomparably the most favourable example of Mohammedan rule is to be found in the Empire of the Great Moguls. The greatest man of that illustrious dynasty as far surpasses the best Caliphs of Cordova, as they excel the Shahs of Persia. The wise and noble Akbar, the third Mogul Emperor, presents to us the extraordinary spectacle of an Oriental despot, who during a long reign of nearly half a century was unblemished by a single crime worthy of record. In warfare he was humane, forbidding the sale of captives as slaves, dispensing when possible with the punishment of death, and forbidding it to be inflicted with unnecessary pain, or prolonged torture. In legislation he was liberal; he abolished the capitation tax hitherto imposed upon the Hindoos, he admitted men of all creeds to the highest offices of state. But, unfortunately, it cannot be maintained that this splendid example of an enlightened Moslem ruler was himself a veritable Mussulman. He was in fact an eclectic, and, beyond the doctrine of the unity of God, he paid but little attention to the teaching, theological or practical, of the Koran. He treated Christianity with marked respect, and even permitted one of his sons to be instructed in the Gospel. The Moslem, too, was free to drink wine, to eat pork, to play at dice, and to withdraw, if he pleased, from the Mosque. In short, Akbar was so sorry a Mussulman that he incurred the displeasure of his Moslem subjects, not, we may suppose, so much from the indulgences which he allowed to them, as for the lenity and impartial justice which he observed towards all other creeds. None of his successors were equally tolerant, and in Aurungzebe Moslem bigotry again mounted the throne. The mild and equitable rule of Akbar is emphatically the case of an exception which proves the rule. Still it is to be freely granted that the lot of the Hindoos under Mussulman rule in India has never been so unhappy as the lot of the subject Christians in other countries. While this has been partly due to the character of the rulers, much, no doubt, has been owing also to the character of the ruled. The Hindoo was naturally more passive and submissive than the native of western countries, and the mild tolerance of his religious creed inspired him with no earnest zeal either to propagate his own faith, or to resist the faith of his conquerors.

But if there have been a few Moslem dynasties which present some passing gleams, more or less bright, more or less prolonged, of civilisation and righteous government, there is one which, from the beginning of its career to the present day, has acted the part of the destroyer and the oppressor with the most fearful and unrelenting consistency. No country under Moslem rule is permanently prosperous, but the Ottoman Turk has succeeded beyond all others who have professed the faith of Islam in making the countries subject to his rule permanently miserable. The land may be 'as the Garden of Eden before him, but behind him it is a desolate wilderness.' There is no country, perhaps, which Providence has blessed with a more bountiful store of natural resources than Asia Minor, especially on the sea coast; its rivers ran with gold, its mountains yielded copper and iron, and costly marble; its plains waved with all manner of crops, and the sides of its hills were clad with the vine and the olive. In the days of Greek and Roman enterprise the coast was thickly studded with populous and opulent cities. Under the care of an industrious people, it once was, and might be again, a paradise of beauty, and a treasure house of wealth. But now the traveller wanders through a dreary region rich only in ruins, the melancholy relics of departed splendour, and inhabited only by roving bands of Turcomans, and their herds of goats. Travellers also in Palestine tell us that the sacred soil would be prodigal in its gifts; that it might be again 'a land of wheat, and barley, and vines and fig trees and pomegranates, a land of oil olive and honey; a land wherein men might eat bread without scarceness; they should not lack anything in it; a land whose stones are iron, and out of whose hills men might dig brass;'[1] but the curse of Turkish Mohammedan occupation is upon it, and, save in the neighbourhood of Christian villages, the once fruitful land has become barren. The condition of European Turkey is too notorious, unhappily, at the present time to require any description or comment. The conclusion to which we are brought by this rapid survey is that sooner or later, in less degree or in greater, historians and travellers have the same tale to tell of all countries under Moslem rule—the tale of lost fertility of the soil, of a diminished and degraded population, of ruined towns, of poverty-stricken villages.

Turning now from the effect of Mohammedanism upon the countries where it was introduced to its effect on human character, some analogy is, I think, discernible between

[1] See especially Captain Warren's 'Underground Jerusalem,' chap. xx.

the two. The immediate effect is surprisingly great, and for the most part exceedingly admirable, but it does not last. The first successors of Mahomet himself were splendid examples of the character which his religion could produce. Abu Bakr and Omar, Othman and Ali, were patterns of temperance, justice, and honour, for parallels to whom we look in vain among the corrupt and effete rulers of the Roman Empire in their day. But this early and speedy promise is followed by a no less rapid deterioration and decay. In the course of a few generations the noble breed of men who founded the Empire of Islam, partly warriors, partly statesmen, partly even saints, has vanished away. The Christians in the Syrian province of the Roman Empire almost welcomed their Saracenic conquerors as affording them the prospect of a happier lot than that which they endured under the evil administration of a decadent power; but in a few generations these hopes were frustrated: the conquerors became oppressors, and the province was transformed into a desert. In like manner the earlier Ottoman princes, although never approaching the Saracenic Caliphs in nobility of character, were not destitute of many fine qualities, and Othman at least had some true notions about the duties and obligations of a sovereign to his people. 'Rule mercifully and justly,' were the last words he spoke to his son. But his successors quickly degenerated into merciless tyrants, and have finally dwindled into the abject and despicable creatures whom we have now beheld for generations, seated on the throne of Constantinople, and in whom it is often difficult to say whether wickedness or weakness is the more distinctive feature.

With regard to the science, literature, and art of the Saracens, of which one hears and reads so much, I would not for a moment question their reality or underrate their value; but that they were in any sense direct products of Islam is, I think, very much to be doubted. Where did the Saracens get these things? Did they evolve them from their 'own inner consciousness'? They certainly did not bring them with them from Mecca and Medina. The fact is, that though they succeeded in destroying much of Greek and Roman literature and art, they could not destroy all. They could not destroy every copy of Aristotle and Hippocrates: they could not break down every Roman arch, nor did they demolish the mighty dome of St. Sophia at Constantinople. And there were men among the Arabs who were wise enough to study these Greek and Roman masterpieces of thought and art, and clever enough to turn their study to good practical account. They taught in Persia and in the Western part of the Roman Empire what they had learned in the Eastern part of it; and reproduced, perhaps with improvements, in Cordova or Bagdad, what they had seen in Byzantium. Their range of study amongst Greek authors was limited, and confined to translations of books on physical and metaphysical science. The research of Gibbon failed to discover a record of any Arabic translation of any Greek poet, orator, or historian. We cannot rate very highly the literary genius of a people who neglected the richest treasury of human thought in these departments which the world possesses. Their native literary productions may be of a very high order; but it is difficult to believe that what is so very insignificant in translation, can be positively first rate in the original, at least in matter, though it may be in style. Of the value of Arabian contributions to astronomy, mathematics, and medicine, I am quite incompetent to decide. Astronomy, we may say, is indigenous in the East, where the climate favours and facilitates the study. The so-called Arabic numerals appear to be of Indian origin.

If, then, it be true that the Mohammedans picked up their science and art, for the most part second-hand, from those fragments of both in the Roman Empire which escaped destruction from the early Mohammedan invaders, this question naturally occurs :—supposing Eastern and Western Christianity had been left to pursue their course unmolested in Syria, Palestine, Asia Minor, Egypt, Northern Africa, Spain, and Turkey, would not science, literature, the arts, and everything else which makes up civilisation, have flourished as well as they have done in those countries under Moslem rule, or do now in those whose are still under it? It is hard to believe that they would not have flourished, not only as well, but a great deal better. At any rate, they could not have flourished less than they do in most of those countries at the present moment. Mr. Palgrave bears strong testimony to the high intellectual and practical qualities of the Arabs; he sees capacities and aptitudes in the race for accomplishing great things in science and art, but he adds: 'When the Koran and Mecca shall have disappeared from Arabia, then, and then only, can we expect to see the Arab assume that place in the ranks of civilization from which Mahomet and his book have, more than any other cause, long held him back.' Here again, then, we see, as in the case of Persia, that Islam left to itself has somehow the unpleasant knack of consuming energy and retarding progress.

And this brings me to the last point in connection with this part of our subject. As the greatest and noblest specimen of a so-called Mohammedan sovereign, Akbar, was not, strictly speaking, a Mohammedan at all, so we find that, in all Mohammedan states, many of the most eminent men in all departments, politics, war, and literature, belonged, originally at least, to an alien race, and an alien creed, most commonly Christian or Jewish.[1] The most remarkable illustration of this fact, because it is one which lasted for several centuries, was the employment by the Ottoman Turks of the corps known by the name of the Janissaries. From the end of the fourteenth up to the middle of the seventeenth century, the great military conquests of the Turks were mainly due to this celebrated

[1] He who thinks it worth while to plod through the lists of learned men in the pages of Abdulpharagius may soon convince himself of this fact.

body of soldiers. And who were the Janissaries? They were the offspring of Christians in the provinces which the Turk had already subdued—Greece, Albania, Bulgaria, and Roumania. They were a human tax levied by the conqueror on his victims; the very flower of their strength. Torn at an early age from their homes, they were carefully trained up as Mussulmans, in ignorance of any home but the camp, and of any earthly power to whom allegiance was due, save the representative of the great prophet of Islam. 'From the seminaries of the Janissaries,' says Von Hammer, 'issued the greatest men of the Ottoman Empire. As long as the yearly levy of Christian children continued, their most famous statesmen and generals were for the most part born Greeks, Albanians, and Bosnians; seldom native Turks.' 'And thus,' he proceeds in cogent and indignant language, 'thus the strength of Turkish despotism repaired itself in the heart-blood of Christendom; and by means of this cunning engine of statecraft Greece was compelled to tear herself to pieces by the hands of her own children.' The words of Von Hammer are only a repetition of an observation made centuries before, in 1573, by a Venetian diplomatist at the court of Selim II. 'It is in the highest degree remarkable,' he said, 'that the wealth, the administration, the force, in short the whole body politic of the Ottoman Empire rests upon, and is entrusted to, men born in the Christian faith, converted into slaves, and reared up as Mahometans.' The saying remains in a great measure true to the present day. Whatever vital energy there is in Turkey, whatever agricultural industry, whatever commercial enterprise, appears to depend upon Jews or Christians; in fact upon any people but the Turks; and though the common Turk can fight with courageous obstinacy, the conduct of the fleet and army of that poor shadowy thing men call the Sublime Porte, appears to be entrusted in a great measure to foreigners. We do not say that the barbarism of the Turk is the product of Islam; far from it. It is, no doubt, in a great measure inherent in the Tartar race; but we do say that Mohammedanism has not cured it, or even improved it. As he was barbarian in the beginning, so is the Turk barbarian now, and so, as long as he remains Mohammedan, barbarian to all human appearance he will continue to be. On the other hand, experience warrants the assertion that there is no race, barbarian or civilised, of which Christianity has taken a *firm hold*,[1] that has not advanced, and that does not manifest capacities of further progress to an indefinite extent. This is the real answer to those superficial remarks often made that the Russian or the Bulgarian is as barbarous as the Turk, that the Turk 'is a gentleman,' and so on. It is not indeed true, even now; but if it were true, we might be quite sure that it would not remain true, because history and experience teach us, that while in Chris-

[1] I use these words advisedly because Abyssinia is an instance of a state which has long professed Christianity, and yet is barbarous; but Christianity in Abyssinia is so very imperfect and impure that it can hardly be said to have more than *touched* it.

tian states, there is an indefinite power of advance, Mohammedan states, after quickly reaching a certain point, become stationary, or else retrograde. In the most degraded, the most barbarian Christian state, there are untold germs, endless possibilities of growth. Is it thus with Mohammedan nations? Let the past history or the present condition of Arabia, of Persia, of Syria, of Egypt, of Northern Africa, of Spain, of Asia Minor, of Turkey in Europe supply the answer. It is easy to point to individual Mohammedans who have been better than individual Christians, just as it is easy to point to special eras when some Mohammedan states have been more civilised than some Christian states. But this proves nothing. The question is, not whether Islam has produced here and there fine types of character, or splendid eras of civilisation, but whether, as a system, in the long run, it promotes a higher and ever increasing order of civilisation and virtue. Are Mohammedan countries, as a rule, prosperous and progressive, or are they depressed, stationary, retrograde? Take a practical test. Would any one as willingly live in the London, the Paris, the Vienna, the St. Petersburg, of 200 years ago, as he would live in the London, the Paris, the Vienna, the St. Petersburg of the present day, notwithstanding all the abominations which yet remain there? I trow not. This is because the countries of which those cities are the capitals have advanced in civilisation. Could we apply the same test with equal confidence to cities under Mohammedan rule, Smyrna, for instance? In fact, from a review of the past history, and a survey of the present condition, of the principal countries in the world, there seems no escape from the conclusion that Christianity and real civilisation are practically co-extensive; where the one ends, the other ends also.

And if this be the case; if, though with occasional gleams of sunshine, the presence of Mohammedanism acts like an east wind on prosperity and progress, the question yet remains *why* is this? The explanation may be found in the fact that three of the worst elements of barbarism, three conditions the most fatal to human civilisation and moral improvement, are incorporated in Islam as integral parts of the system. The three evils to which I allude are polygamy, despotism, and its counterpart, slavery. They are indigenous in the East; Mahomet alleviated them indeed, but they are distinctly adopted in the Koran, and consequently are invested with a kind of divine sanction. They stamp upon the religion of Mahomet an essentially Oriental character. Christianity and the Western nations abhor and repudiate these three evil things, and consequently Mohammedanism has ever been the most implacable foe to Christianity and the Western nations, the most impervious barrier to the advance of Christianity and Western civilisation in an eastward direction.

The establishment of a regulated polygamy by Mahomet was, of course, a great advance upon the unrestrained licentiousness which in Arabia had preceded it; but then polygamy, although controlled, *is* established, with all its concomitant evils: degradation on the side of the woman who belongs to the husband, while the husband does not belong to her: jealousies on both sides, an overgrown and divided household. Yet all who acknowledge the Koran must accept polygamy as a divinely sanctioned condition of life. Under the law of Moses, polygamy was tolerated; under the law of Mahomet it is established. All honour to him for endeavouring to mitigate its evils by restriction. The practice was so deeply rooted in Oriental life, that this was probably all which he could venture to attempt. The divine wisdom of the Mosaic law is manifested in the fact that while it seems to do less for the evil, while it tolerates and places no defined limitations on the practice, it thereby left the way more clear for its ultimate abolition.

To the votary of Islam, again, there is no escape from the recognition of absolute despotism as a divinely ordered form of government. By virtue of his alleged commission from God, Mahomet claimed the right to regulate every item in the life of his disciples; and his successors are suffered to inherit his divine right of absolute power, only limited in their case by deference to the directions of the Koran. That sacred volume is the only groundwork of jurisprudence for nations professing the faith of Islam. It is for the Mussulman his code of civil law, as well as of theology and ethics. The ultimate appeal in every question of law in any Mohammedan nation, whether it be in the East or the West, whether it be in the ninth century or the nineteenth, is to some sentences inscribed on a palm leaf or mutton bone in Arabia in the middle of the seventh century. The rigidity of the Koran is often so incapable of adaptation to the necessities of particular cases that, in order to prevent a deadlock, an ingenious method of evasion is adopted. To quote the words of Gibbon: 'The Kadi respectfully places the sacred volume on his head, and substitutes a dexterous interpretation more apposite to the principles of equity, and to the manners and policy of the times.' Should the employment of this subterfuge become more common, as in some Mohammedan countries seems probable, the way will be indefinitely opened to moral and social, if not religious reformation; but then Islam will cease to be Islam. Where the religion of Mahomet is maintained in its integrity, the sciences of divinity and law coalesce; the jurist and divine is the same person, only looked at from different points of view, and one name is common to him in both capacities. In like manner the functions of monarch and chief pontiff are united in the same person. Such is the impotence of the Ottoman Sultans at the present day, that the administration of government (if the word government can be so far dishonored as to be applied to what is, in fact, merely a system of rapine) must practically be conducted by other wills than theirs; yet the Grand Vizier and the Mufti are in theory only the ministers, and obedient slaves of the Sultan's will in temporal and ecclesiastical affairs. And in the early days of Saracenic and Turkish power, the great Caliphs and Sultans exercised a despotic power exceeding that of any Roman Emperor or Pope; for the will even of the most despotic emperors or popes was subject to the control of some forms of constitutional law, and that law, again, was leavened more or less by the principles of the Gospel. Even the tyranny of the first Buonaparte was not that purely arbitrary will, that mere personal agency, which in its origin is essentially Oriental, and which is embodied in the religious system of Mahomet.

In describing the effects of the early Saracenic conquests, Mr. Finlay remarks: 'No attempt was made to arrange any systematic form of political government, and the whole power of the state was vested in the hands of the chief priest of the religion, who was only answerable for the due exercise of this extraordinary power to God, his own conscience, and the patience of his subjects. The moment, therefore, that the responsibility created by national feelings, military companionship, and exalted enthusiasm ceased to operate on the minds of the Caliphs, the administration became far more oppressive than that of the Roman Empire. No local magistrates elected by the people, and no parish priests connected by their feelings and interests both with their superiors and inferiors, bound society together by common ties; and no system of legal administration, independent of the military and financial authorities, preserved the property of the people from the rapacity of the government. Socially and politically the Saracen Empire was little better than the Gothic, Hunnish, and Avar monarchies; and that it proved more durable with almost equal oppression is to be attributed to the powerful enthusiasm of Mahomet's religion which tempered for some time its avarice and tyranny.' We may add, that where the conscience of the sovereign and the patience of the people are the only bounds to the exercise of his power, conscience is apt to become hardened, and patience amazingly enduring. Inured to subjection, and deprived of any ready means of discussing their wrongs, or concerting resistance, the people are apt to lapse into apathetic indolence, and stupid resignation.

It is unnecessary to add that where polygamy and depotism exist, there also slavery must be found. Slavery, in fact, pervades the whole social and political life of a people under Moslem rule. The wife is the slave of the husband rather than his partner; the domestic servant is the slave of both. The Pasha is the slave of the despot; he is a despot himself over the province which is in bondage to his rule. Slavery appears to be mild in Mohammedan countries, and so it is; not only because kind treatment of the slave is enjoined in the Koran, but also because where all are reduced more or less to the condition of slaves, servitude is no disgrace. Where all are equally subject to the absolute will of the monarch, the sharp distinctions of rank are removed. Servitude becomes no barrier to the elevation of a man to the highest offices in the State. The favour of the despot indeed is more likely to be bestowed on a slave than on a man of noble origin; the policy of the despot being to depress the aristocracy, who might by their position become leaders of rebellion, and to reduce all ranks as much as possible to one dead level of subjection. And, as a matter of fact, the men who have risen to the highest offices in Moslem States, especially at Constantinople, have been commonly men who began by discharging the most menial and often the basest and most disgraceful functions about the court of the sovereign.

We repeat that we do not affirm these evils to be the direct *products* of Islam. They are indigenous in the East, and are deeply rooted in Oriental habits of life; but we do say that they are the concomitants of Islam; that where Islam is established they are established, and further that, though alleviated in degree, they are more closely riveted upon Mohammedan countries than any others, because they are there invested with a divine sanction. Islam has taken up into itself and consecrated these evil forms of Oriental life, and consequently it opposes the most solid obstacle to the reception in the East of Christian and Western civilisation. Where, on the other hand, the Mussulman rules over a population which is Christian and European, he can never assimilate them or be assimilated by them; the Koran forbids him to treat an infidel as his equal; the alien invader can maintain his conquest only by becoming an oppressor; the two elements may live centuries side by side, but like oil and vinegar they will not fuse: the one is Mohammedan, Asiatic, stationary; the other Christian, European, progressive.

As the character of the Great Head of the Christian Church, when He became incarnate, was Catholic, so is the character of the Church which He founded. It is capable of adaptation to human nature everywhere, because it is not like an inanimate machine which, once made, can work only in one way, but is a living organism instinct with a divine life, even the spirit of its Head. It can move in a hundred different ways according to His direction, and accommodate itself to every race, and to every form of social or political condition; it can live under a despotism or are public, amongst the rich and the poor, the Teuton, the Celt, the African, the Indian, the Melanesian. On the other hand as the character of the founder of Islam was essentially Oriental, so is the character of the religion which he founded; it is acceptable to the Oriental nature, but repugnant to the Wcstern; it has made rapid progress and obtained a firm footing among Eastern countries; and, as it will not easily recede from its pretensions to the possession of absolute truth it is the most formidable rival which Christianity has to encounter in the East.

And what tone, it may bc asked, ought the Christian Church to assume towards its rival? Certainly not that of denunciation or defiance, nor, on the other hand, of approbation and concession. In the face of the fact that Christians never have been able to live peaceably and happily under Moslem rule, although at the present day Mussulmans live in great peace and prosperity under Christian rule, it is, we think, rather hard that Christians should be reproached as inclined to an attitude of harsh hostility or contempt towards the Moslem faith.[1] By all means let us recognize to the full what was great and noble in Mahomet himself, and in the work which he accomplished; let us recognize to the full all the good which the religion of Mahomet has done, as well as all the evil, all its truth as well as all its error; let us hold out the right hand of fellowship to the Mussulman as a brother, though an erring brother, whom we are bound to honour, to respect, and even to love. But, on the other hand, do not let us disguise or gloss over the fact that there is error, and most mischievous error in his religion; do not let us talk of it as if it were almost as good as

[1] Bos. Smith, Lect. iv. p. 259, 279, and Preface to second edition, p. 9.

Christianity, or because Mahomet had a sort of reverence for Christ, go to the ridiculous length of calling Islam 'a form of Christianity;'[1] although it expressly denies the very essence of Christianity, the Divinity and Incarnation of our blessed Lord. Do not let us make apologies for praying that the Mussulman may be brought to the knowledge of a nobler and purer faith than his own as if it was an insult.[2] To cultivate friendship and good-will with men of a different creed it cannot be necessary, because it cannot be right, to surrender one jot or tittle of the essential principles of our own faith; conscientious unbelievers would despise us if we did. What is needed is the exercise of that large-hearted charity which seeks their good in every possible way; endeavors to win them to the truth; acts with them where it can, and, where it cannot, stands respectfully and courteously aside. It was a common saying of one of the most uncom-

[1] Bos. Smith, Lect. iv. p. 260.

[2] Ibid. p. 259.

promising Churchmen, the late Dean Hook, to Dissenters with whom he was brought much in contact and always lived on the most friendly terms: 'There is a line between us, but across that line we shake hands.' The saying would equally illustrate the proper attitude of Christians towards the Mussulman, or any other kind of unbeliever. There is a line between us; if we can persuade them to cross the line and to be one with us, we will receive them with open arms; if they will not cross it, let us shake hands over the line, and work hand in hand whenever they will move in a parallel direction with us. But do not let us pretend that there is no line, that Christianity is only a few shades better than Mohammedanism, the Bible only 'as a whole' better than the Koran, and that the difference between the two religions is one not of kind, but only of degree.[1] In short, in our laudable anxiety to make our Christianity pleasant and attractive to men

[1] Bos. Smith, Lect. i., p. 64, 67.

of another creed, let us take heed not to dilute Christian doctrine so far as to find some day that we have lost what was of vital value for ourselves, and only bestowed on others a residuum which was hardly worth their acceptance.